ART BOOKS

FROM CRESCENT MOON PUBLISHING

PERUGINO

PERUGINO

BY SELWYN BRINTON, M.A.

CRESCENT MOON

First published 1912. This edition © 2018.

Printed and bound in the U.S.A.
Set in Book Antiqua 10 on 14pt.
Designed by Radiance Graphics.

Thanks to the authors and publishers quoted.

British Library Cataloguing in Publication data

ISBN-13 9781861716590 (Pbk)
ISBN-13 9781861717139 (Hbk)

CRESCENT MOON PUBLISHING
P.O. Box 1312, Maidstone, Kent, ME14 5XU
Great Britain, www.crmoon.com

CONTENTS

Note On the Text

NOTE ON THE TEXT

The text is from *Perugino* by Selwyn Brinton, published by
Frederick Stokes, New York, 1912.

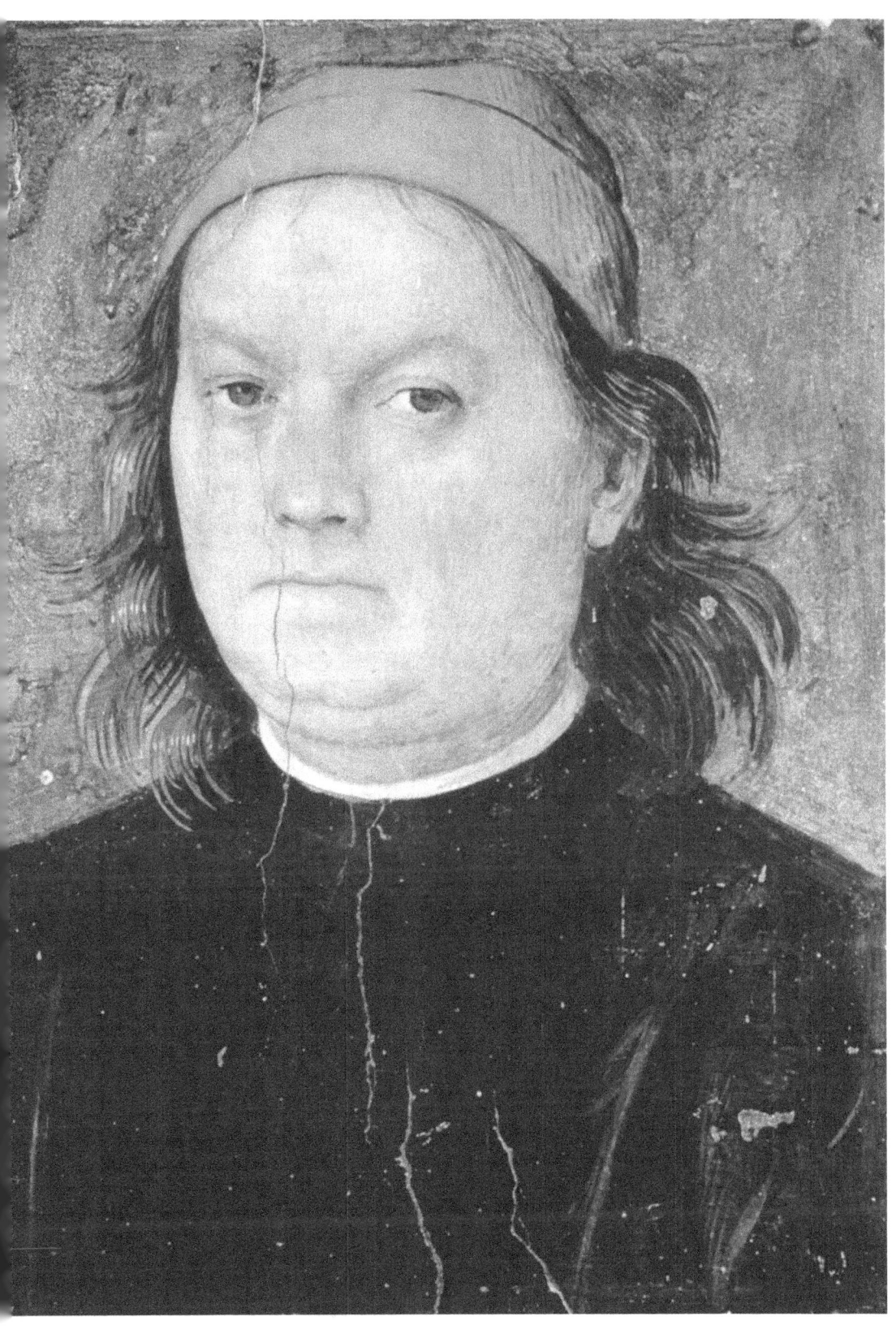

Portrait of Perugino, 1500, Perugia

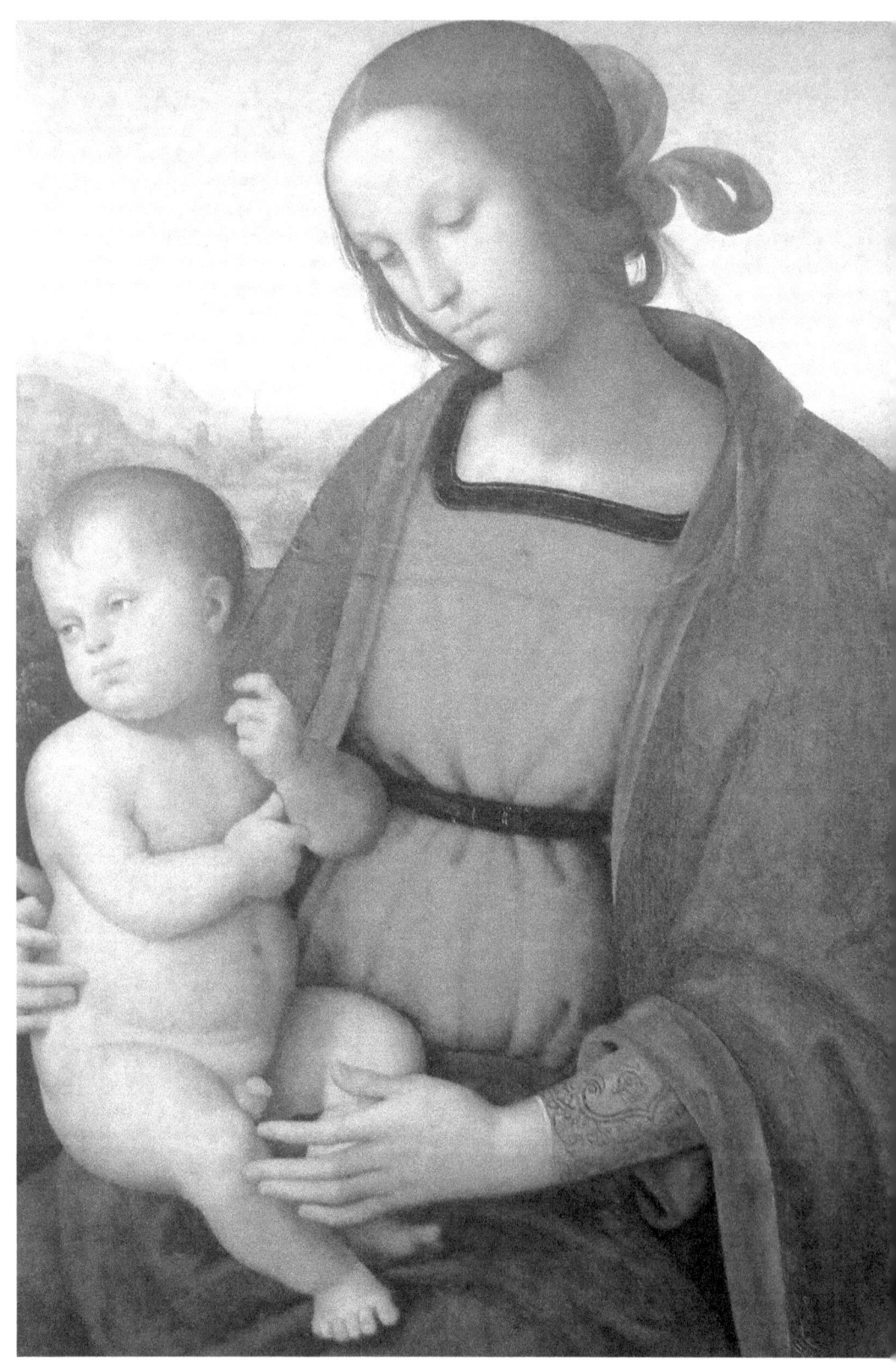

Perugino, Madonna and Child, Washington, DC

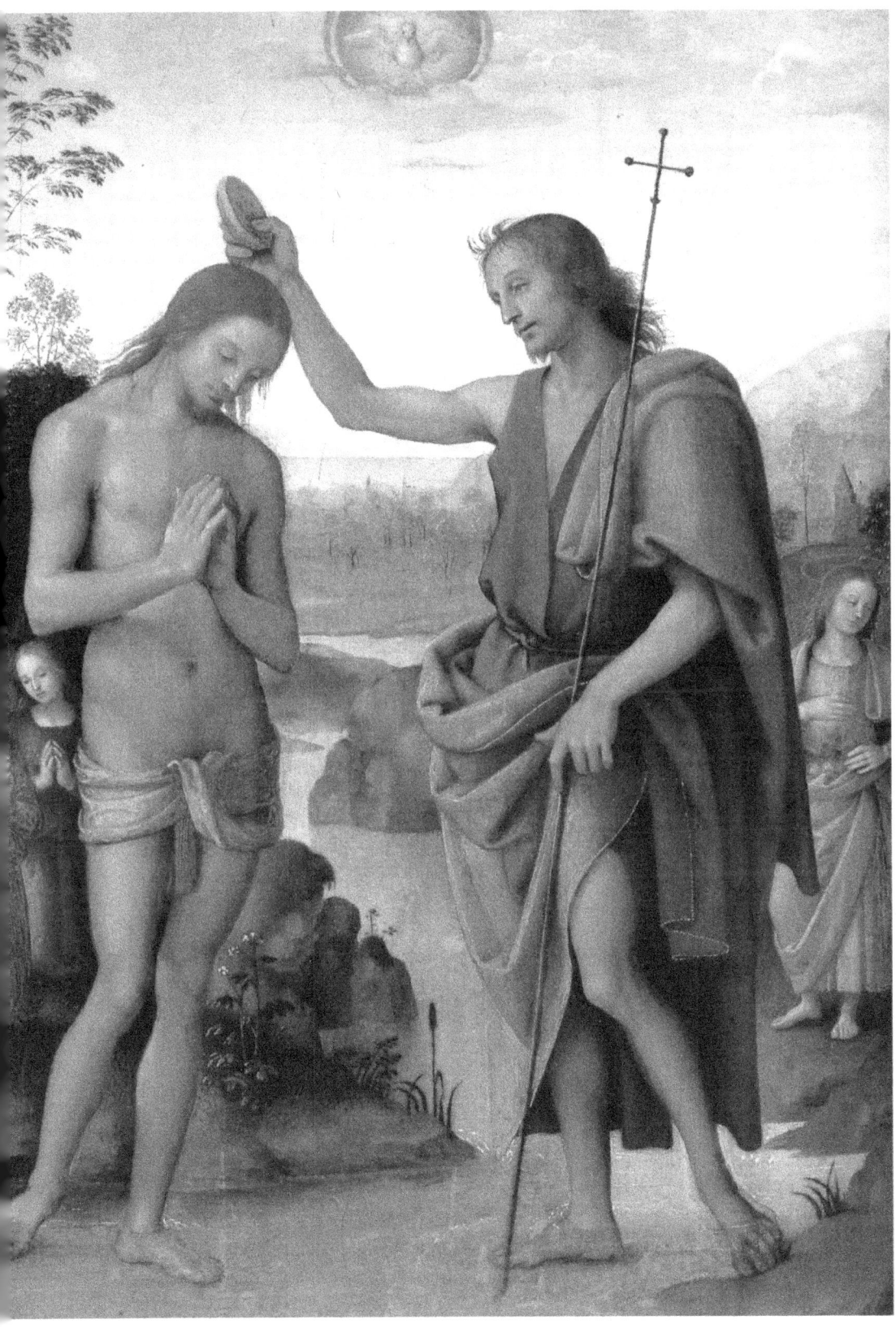

Perugino, The Baptism of Christ, 1498, Vienna

I

In considering the work of one of the greatest of the masters of the Renaissance, we have to go further back than the disputed question as to who was the first teacher of Pietro di Cristofano Vannucci – surnamed by his contemporaries *"il Perugino,"* the Perugian – and to inquire into the more interesting story of his predecessors in that wonderful School of Umbria, on which his art puts, in a certain sense, the seal and completion.

In an earlier work on this subject I traced this school, in its first definite inception, to that grand old religious painter Niccolo da Foligno, whose art may be studied within his native city of Foligno – in his great altar-piece of the church of S. Niccolo – in Perugia, Paris, London, and his fine paintings in the Vatican Gallery at Rome; and in all these works I traced in Niccolo a great master, "archaic but strong in drawing and full of character, possessing just the qualities of the founder of a great school." But upon that school many influences were to stream in, and to affect its progress. The earlier art of Siena, the city of Mary Virgin, intensely emotional and religious in its character, the dignity of Duccio and the Lorenzetti, the grace and delicate beauty of Simone Memmi were among these. Close to Niccolo himself, in the hill-town of Montefalco, the Florentine, Benozzo Gozzoli, pupil of Fra Angelico, had been busied on picture stories from St. Francis' legend, which seem to find their continuation in the Perugian miracle pictures of Fiorenzo di Lorenzo; and yet nearer to Florence, in the Umbrian Borderland, that "King of Painting," Piero della Francesca, was to combine the Umbrian emotion with Florentine intellectualism.

These are the influences which were to stream upon the young Pietro as an eager and industrious student – some among them of course indirectly, but others no doubt very directly and immediately. Vasari's account, which is still of first value save where it is opposed by stronger evidence, is that he was sent as a poor boy to grind colours and run errands in the "bottega" of some Perugian painter. The impression which is here given of his extreme poverty is probably exaggerated. The Vannucci family had enjoyed the citizenship of Perugia since 1427, nor was it in Perugia but in their native township of Castel (later Città) della Pieve that his son Pietro was born to Cristofano Vannucci.

But we may take it that he left the paternal roof while yet a child (he was probably not more than nine years old), and was apprenticed, as above stated, in Perugia – though to what artist Vasari does not tell us. Here, therefore, conjecture is rife, and Buonfigli, – that delightful decorator of the Perugian Palazzo Pubblico, – Fiorenzo di Lorenzo, and even Niccolo da Foligno himself have been assigned by various critics as his teacher. Personally, I incline to Fiorenzo di Lorenzo, whose easel paintings in the Gallery of Perugia seem to foreshadow the typical Perugino background; but it is yet more probable that either as a master or (as suggested by Crowe and Cavalcaselle) as a journeyman associate he may have come under the influence of Piero della Francesca, and gained from him that intimate knowledge of perspective which appears in all his later works.

In any case this unknown master – if we are to believe Vasari – was an inspiring influence; for not only "did he never cease to set before Pietro the great advantages and honours that were to be obtained from painting … but when the boy was wont to frequently inquire of him in what city the best artists were formed … he constantly received the same reply, namely, that Florence was the place above all others wherein men attain to perfection in all the arts, but more especially in painting." I spare to my reader the long harangue which Vasari here puts into the mouth of young Pietro's unknown teacher, and which the critic pretty certainly evolved out of his own inner consciousness; and come to his conclusion, which is, that our Pietro, with every goodwill to improve himself, came to Florence, and entered the famous bottega of Andrea del Verrocchio. Nor do I see any sufficient ground to reject this statement, though Morelli in his "Italian Painters" (vol. i. p. 107) emphasises very properly the importance of his earlier training, "in all probability at Perugia, under Fiorenzo di Lorenzo, and then at Arezzo under Piero della Francesca," and will not have him described "as unconditionally the pupil of Verrocchio." The point to notice here is that Pietro must have been a fairly advanced artist when he went, obviously to "finish" himself, to Florence, and that in his earlier work it is not so much the direct influence of Verrocchio which counts as that of his countrymen, the Umbrians.

But at Florence he must certainly have been in these years, going there (as the author I have just quoted suggests) "soon after 1470," probably, for a time at least, within Verrocchio's workshop, and drinking in all the glorious message of Florentine art in the company of the younger generation of her craftsmen, among whom Giovanni Santi, in his rhyming chronicle of art, mentions directly another pupil of Verrocchio, the young Leonardo da Vinci, as his friend and associate:

"*Due giovin par d'etate e par d'amori*
Leonardo da Vinci e'l Perusino
Pier della Pieve...."

That he must have been already advanced in his art in those days is borne out by the fact that only ten years later (1481) he was summoned by Pope Sixtus to Rome, to decorate, in the company of the great Florentine masters – Ghirlandajo, Cosimo Rosselli, and Botticelli – the walls of the "Sistine" Chapel in fresco.

Prior to this great commission, Milanesi notes (1475) frescoes painted by him in the great hall of the Perugian Palazzo Pubblico, which have entirely disappeared, and others (1478) in a chapel at Cerqueto, of which only a "St. Sebastian," very Umbrian in character, now survives.

> "Whence it came about," says Vasari, "that the fame of Pietro was so spread abroad within Italy and without that, to his great glory, he was brought by Pope Sixtus to work at Rome in his chapel, in company with other excellent craftsmen: in the which place he made the story of Christ where he gives to St. Peter the keys, and likewise the 'Nativity' and 'Baptism of Christ' and the 'Finding of Moses' … and on the side where is the altar the mural painting of the 'Assumption of Madonna,' wherein he drew Pope Sixtus on his knees. But these last-mentioned works were destroyed to make room for the 'Last Judgment' of the divine Michelangelo, in the time of Pope Paul III."

Vasari here refers to the wall paintings in fresco of the "Nativity," "Finding of Moses," and "Assumption." All these have disappeared without a trace.

There remain the magnificent "Delivery of the Keys" and the frescoes of the "Journey of Moses" and the "Baptism of Christ." I made a careful study of these last two frescoes at Rome ten years ago, when writing the life of Pinturicchio, and that study led me to the conclusion that here we have Pinturicchio working under Perugino himself. "The Moses, for instance," I wrote of the "Journey of Moses in Egypt,"

> "who appears here is thoroughly Peruginesque (he is to be compared with the Christ and the Baptist in the fresco opposite), but is painted probably by Pinturicchio under Perugino's instructions. The Zipporah, too, when she is seen advancing, or again where the child in her lap undergoes the rite of circumcision, and the female attendant in white in the corner of the fresco are creations of Vannucci's very type and mould. The beautiful landscape, however, with its palm-trees and overhanging rocks, is thoroughly in Pinturicchio's manner, and the fresco is full of grouped portraits – a Florentine trait…. Now, if we turn about, we can examine the fresco opposite (right wall next the altar) of the 'Baptism of Christ': here again I find the two

Umbrians to have been working in collaboration. In support of this attribution it is interesting to compare the 'Baptism' here with the undoubted 'Baptism' by Perugino at Foligno. I have seen both the Foligno painting and that of the Sistina this month, and have photographs of each before me as I correct these notes; and I find the two groups absolutely identical save for the slight variations in type and drapery of the St. John, caused, as I think, by his having been painted by Pinturicchio, but under the elder master's guidance."

I have here quoted from my notes, written within the Sistine Chapel itself, at some length, because they lead me to some extent to differ from the conclusions of Senator Morelli, who, insisting on the poetry of Pinturicchio's landscapes, is disposed to give both these frescoes to that great master. Pinturicchio was undoubtedly working in Rome as Perugino's assistant during this pontificate of Pope Sixtus. Crowe and Cavalcaselle say of this artist:

"He was a Perugian by birth and education, had followed with moderate talent the lessons of Buonfigli and Fiorenzo di Lorenzo, and afterwards joined the atelier of Perugino. He had all the qualities that should be sought in a subordinate, and might have become indispensable to one who undertook large commissions and required an orderly superintendent for his apprentices. It was natural that Perugino should take him into partnership and give him a third of his profits. Nor do the Sixtine frescoes discountenance the belief that the two men stood in this relation to each other in 1484."

When Perugino left Rome for Florence in 1486, Pinturicchio remained there, obtained commissions from the great families of the Della Rovere and Cibo, and from the Borgia Pope Alexander VI., for whom he decorated the famous "Appartamento Borgia" within the Vatican. He thus began to assume the position of an independent master; but if we trace his hand (especially in the children and landscape backgrounds) in the two Sistine wall paintings which I have just mentioned – though working still under the elder master's supervision and assistance – it is Perugino alone who comes before us, in his full strength, in the "Delivery to St. Peter of the Keys." The subject, it has been well said, was a simple incident, but demanded "from the deep meaning attached to it as related to the history of the Roman church a certain grandeur and solemnity of treatment"; and here at once we see the full influence upon Pietro of his Florentine training, combined, in a very interesting way, with those earlier Umbrian elements which still remained with him as the strongest impulse, and which he had learnt from his earlier Perugian master, or later, not improbably, from the great Piero della Francesca. No writer upon Umbrian art can afford to neglect its wonderful landscape backgrounds, often poetic and fantastic, as in the art of Pinturicchio, but always with this sense of roominess, of vastness, and spaciousness, which Mr. Berenson has very happily defined by the phrase of "space-composition"; and, writing of this very fresco in an earlier work, I compared within the Sistina the crowded frescoes and stir of movement of Botticelli or Cosimo Rosselli with those wide spaces of Perugino's "Granting of the Keys," where our eyes are carried onwards from the central group far away to the distant temple with its roomy porticoes.

But if the background with its Bramantesque temple and the middle distance is still purely Umbrian, and seems to foreshadow the "Sposalizio" at Caen, or at the Brera, in those noble figures grouped upon the front plane of the composition – many of them obviously contemporary portraits (one of them in a skullcap being suggested as the master himself) – we may trace the dominant influence of the great Florentines, of Masaccio within the Brancacci Chapel of the Carmine, and of the noble fresco art of Domenico Ghirlandajo. And thus Pietro Perugino combines within himself already the two most important currents of the art of the Italian Renaissance – that art of Florence, with its intellectualism, its masterly drawing, its sense of form, and that lovely devotional spirit of Umbrian art, developed and inherited from the earlier Sienese. He is at least for us here the precursor – the "forerunner"; and what his divinely gifted pupil, the young Raphael of Urbino, was to complete he already foreshadows.

Another point which has not been brought out very fully by

our master's critics is the predominance of fresco painting in his earlier work. The value of fresco painting to these Italian masters as a training for eye and hand cannot be too much insisted upon. It needed both a sure eye and a quick hand, for the painting had to be done at once when the plaster was ready to receive it; and there can be no doubt that Pietro's absolute mastery, at this period, of this difficult art had prepared him for the wonderful series of altar-pieces in the tempera and oil mediums which we are now about to study.

Perugino, as we have noticed, had returned to Florence in the autumn of 1486, when the frescoes of the Sistine Chapel were no doubt completed, and soon after this (1489) received an invitation to visit Orvieto – his altar-piece for S. Domenico at Fiesole having been completed in the year previous. The frescoes in the Capella di S. Brizio within Orvieto Cathedral had been left unfinished through the death of Fra Angelico, and our Perugino, as a master "whose fame had been spread throughout Italy," was now requested to examine the chapel and tender for the completion of its decoration. He did so, but his price was a high one – 1500 ducats and all materials to be found him – and we shall trace later how the negotiations, protracted for several years, came eventually to nothing.

For the moment Florence attracted him, for here, in January of 1491, under the presidency of Lorenzo de' Medici, called the Magnificent, the foremost artists of the day were gathered to consider the decoration of the façade of the Florentine Duomo; and here Perugino was present, beside such masters as Domenico Ghirlandajo, Cosimo Rosselli, Andrea della Robbia, Botticelli, Baldovinetti, Pollajuolo – a long list of names now world-famed in the story of art. From Florence, in March of this same year, our master made his way to Perugia, where he drew the balance of his pay for the Sistine frescoes; and then, prudently avoiding Orvieto, went on south to Rome, where we have seen that Pinturicchio had now established himself, together with the Florentine Filippino Lippi, and had found many commissions.

But Perugino soon found a patron in the Cardinal Giuliano della Rovere, later to become famous in history as Pope Julius II.; and this powerful prelate protected our artist from the importunities of the Orvietans, who were pressing him to fulfil his contract, and threatening, if he delayed longer, to appoint another artist in his place. Cardinal Giuliano, the imperious patron later of Michelangelo, took the matter with a characteristically high hand. "We laboured under the impression" – thus he writes to the Council of Orvieto – "that you were to be compliant, as best suits the love we have ever borne to your community. And so we now again exhort and pray that you do reserve the place which is his due to Maestro Pietro, and refrain from molesting him…."

The fact was that the great prelate wanted Pietro for a time for himself, and to this time (1491) belongs the lovely altar-piece, formerly in the Cardinal's Palace, and now in the Villa Albani at Rome. All our master's devotional feeling, his refinement and beauty of type, his wealth of golden colour, is found already in this wonderful altar-piece, which is divided into six compart-ments, the central panel being occupied by the "Nativity," with above the "Crucifixion" and "Annunciation," and at the sides the figures of four adoring saints. The landscape background is here of extraordinary beauty, reflecting the quiet serenity of the kneeling figures, and on the pillars of the colonnade behind the "Nativity" the master has signed his work –

PETRUS DE PERUSIA PINXIT 1491.

The Albani altar-piece had always ranked as one of Perugino's loveliest and most typical creations, worthy to stand beside the beautiful altar-piece of the Certosa of Pavia, of which England is now the fortunate possessor in her National Gallery; but to this busy and fertile period in the master's career belong a number of attractive and interesting works, which we must now endeavour in some measure to classify and analyse.

I have already alluded to the altar-piece of S. Domenico at

Fiesole; but Pietro painted another altar-piece for the same church in 1493, which is now in the Uffizi Gallery, a "Virgin Enthroned," between Saints Sebastian and John Baptist, dated and signed, as usual, "Petrus Perusinus." The "Crucifixion" of La Calza (Florence), showing very markedly the influence of Luca Signorelli, may have probably preceded this; but to the same year of 1493 belongs the beautiful "Pietà" (Dead Christ) of the Florence Accademia, and the wonderful and most impressive "Crucifixion" of S. Maria Maddalena de' Pazzi (Florence) was commissioned by Pietro Pucci in 1493, though it was not completed till April of 1496. Unsurpassed here is the master in the solemnity, the sense of aloofness from earthly things, which he conveys to us in these six figures – the Crucified, with as spectators His mother, the beloved disciple, and kneeling saints, seen against the wide stretch of such an Umbrian background as we may see from Perugia or Cortona or Assisi; and next in importance to this masterpiece of religious art is the famous "Pietà" of S. Chiara, of which Vasari speaks with such enthusiasm.

> "He worked out for the ladies of Santa Chiara a painting of the dead Christ, with colouring so lovely and so fresh that by good craftsmen it was held a thing marvellous and excellent. In this work certain very lovely heads of old men are to be seen, and likewise certain Maries who, with weeping faces, regard the dead man with reverence and wondrous love; and moreover he made a landscape which was then highly esteemed. It is said that Francesco del Pugliese would fain have given to the aforesaid nuns three times as much money as they had paid to Pietro, and in addition offered to give them a similar painting made by the artist's own hand; and they would not agree, because Pietro said that he could never equal that original."

This noble creation of religious art is now in the Pitti Palace at Florence, and fully bears out Vasari's appreciative criticism: in composition, in beauty of type in the mourning women and men, in the lax body of the dead Saviour, in the exquisite landscape with its trees defined against the far sky, our master touches here a very high level in religious art. As usual with works of this importance he fully signed it, on the rock on which the Christ is laid –

PETRUS PERUSINUS PINXIT A.D.
MCCCCLXXXXV;

and the very careful studies which he made for the groups in this picture may be seen among the drawings of the Uffizi collection.

When we consider that the magnificently virile portrait of Francesco delle Opere (1494), now in the Tribuna of the Uffizi, belongs to this same period, as well as the lovely "Madonna with Saints" of S. Agostino at Cremona (1494, signed and dated), the "Ascension of Christ," painted for S. Pietro at Perugia (1495, now at Lyons Hôtel de Ville), and the grand altar-piece of the Vatican (1496), which I shall describe more fully later, we shall agree with the critics (Crowe and Cavalcaselle), who describe the year 1495 as "remarkable in the career of Vannucci. It was that in which an Umbrian ... successfully applied the laws of composition and added a calm tenderness to the gravity of the Florentine school; and through his influence on Fra Bartolommeo and Raphael replaced, as far as it was possible, the pious mysticism that had perished with Angelico." The master's influence on Fra Bartolommeo may be clearly traced in the "Pietà" of S. Chiara, the forerunner of the Frate's own noble work; and it was not far from this very time (1495) that the young Rafaelle Sanzio must have entered his Perugian workshop.

II

We have now traced the art of Pietro Vannucci from its first beginnings in the workshop of some unknown teacher at Perugia to the time when he was one of the accepted masters of Italian art, as much at home in Florence – that glowing centre of artistic impulse and creation – as in his own Perugia, or in the Rome of the Renaissance Popes. Here, then, before we proceed further with the story of his art, which is practically the story of his busy life, there are some points on which we shall not waste time in lingering. We saw how Perugino, like Giotto himself and almost every great master of Italian painting, had perfected his knowledge and trained his eye and hand in the practice of fresco-painting; and we have next to notice that he obtained fame among his contemporaries, as well as patronage, from his knowledge and use of the new oil medium. Vasari on this point is most explicit: "Certainly colouring was a matter which Pietro thoroughly understood, and this both in fresco as well as in oil ..." and again he mentions certain pictures specially as being painted in oil.

Of course one cannot set up even such direct evidence from Vasari as conclusive, for we know there are many slips in his invaluable chronicle; and this very point of the master's medium for his panel pictures has been questioned by modern critics.

Dr. G. C. Williamson in his excellent monograph on Perugino

refers to Mr. Herbert Horne – a critic whose opinion on Italian art carries great weight – as saying that "all Perugino's pictures were painted in tempera on a gesso background," and suggests at least that an entirely different technique can be traced in the Albani altar-piece and that of the Certosa. Crowe and Cavalcaselle, in their notice of Perugino, have analysed very carefully his technique, and shown how his flesh tints were worked up from a warm brown undertone, through a succession of glazes, each lighter in colour and fuller in body than the last, "receiving light from without and transparency from within," till the highest light was reached.

In this analysis the authors have obviously and entirely the oil medium in view; but there is another view which, as it seems to me, may throw light upon the question.

Experiments have, as I understand, been made in late years in Germany to combine the use of tempera with that of oil-painting – the object being to combine the brilliancy and richness of oil with the lasting colour of tempera, in which yolk of egg was used with the pure colours – and I believe that certain results have been attained. Now this was just the position of painting in Perugino's day, when upon the old tempera panels of the Giottesques and their successors the oil technique of the Van Eycks was asserting its advantages; and I would suggest that our master in this period of transition used both mediums, and perhaps sometimes in the same picture may have passed from one to the other. Here, too, his connection with the Gesuati may have aided him materially, for Vasari tells us expressly how these friars, for whom he worked very frequently, were practised in the art of colours as well as enamel and glass-painting, and it was perhaps from them that he had learned the secret which makes his altar-pieces still so transparent and so pure in colour.

Another point which we cannot fail to notice at this period of Pietro's life is his immense activity, his careful business relations in contracts for his work, and his continual industry. He is so constantly on the move that we begin to wonder how he found time for his paintings: he is so continually productive that we wonder no less that he found it possible to travel. His wanderings might be normal in these days of Pullman-cars and express trains, but in an age when any journey was a matter of difficulty and often personal danger they seem almost phenomenal. From Orvieto (1490) he goes to Florence, from Florence to Perugia, and thence to Rome; in 1493 he is married at Fiesole to Chiara Fancelli; in 1494 he is at Venice, and probably at Cremona, painting there his altar-piece at S. Agostino; then back again to Florence, at Perugia in March of 1496, making his contract for the famous Vatican Madonna, and at Pavia in October of the same year, working at his no less famous altar-piece of the Certosa.

In all these visits he was either arranging for fresh work or leaving some lovely altar-piece as a memorial of his presence; and next we shall notice that the two real points of attraction in all this busy life are Perugia, his native city, if not actually his birthplace, and Florence. Rome, though he spent some time there, and completed much important work, never, I think, had the same hold upon him; but between Florence and Perugia he often seems to hesitate. And this is really important, because the two tendencies, the Umbrian and the Florentine, are always present in his art. He had completed, as we saw, his training in the city of Arno, had married later (1493) a beautiful Florentine girl, the daughter of Luca Fancelli, who brought with her a dowry of 500 golden florins, and on his return from Perugia in 1496 had invested part of the money he had received for his altar-piece of the Magistrates' Chapel in land at Florence.

In fact, during the whole of these years, after his return from Rome at the time of Alexander Borgia's accession (1492) to nearly 1500, I take our master's real centre of activity as being Florence; there he had his workshop, painted panels for distant customers, undertook frescoes for the Florentine convents, and returned after his business visits to other parts of Italy. The year 1499 marks a change in all this, for this was the year in which the master definitely threw over the offer of the Orvietans to decorate their

Capella di S. Brizio in Orvieto Duomo, and accepted his great commission from the Perugian guild of bankers to adorn with fresco paintings their audience-hall – the Sala del Cambio. This great commission necessitated a long stay at Perugia, and therefore the master broke up his Florentine workshop, or "bottega."

But Florence had evidently a very deep hold on his affections, for we find that in 1504 he gave up his Perugian establishment for the purpose of returning to Florence, and on arriving there took a lodging in the Pinti suburb. At Florence Perugino was justly esteemed as one of the great master-craftsmen of the city, and as such was invariably consulted – as in the great meeting held (January of 1491) to consider the new façade of S. Maria del Fiore; or again when (in January of 1497) he was invited with Benozzo Gozzoli, Cosimo Rosselli, and Filippino Lippi to value the frescoes of Alessio Baldovinetti in S. Trinità of Florence; or yet again when (June of 1498), after the destruction of the lantern of S. Maria del Fiore by lightning, he tendered his advice along with Filippino and Lorenzo di Credi.

But while Pietro had been busied at Perugia, in those years of absence (1499-1504) a new spirit, of dæmonic power, had come to fascinate the Florentines, and give them a new conception of the art of the human form; and, in fact, hardly had our master reached Florence and secured his lodging than he was invited to give his verdict as to the best site for Michelangelo's gigantic marble "David." Feeling ran high in the city both as to the site and the work itself. As to the former, the Loggia de' Signori was suggested, but Michelangelo himself preferred the left-hand side of the doorway of the Palazzo Vecchio, and his wish was respected. Yet the feeling against this figure among some of the citizens was such that, when it was exposed, it became a mark for missiles, and the watchmen set to guard it were assaulted. We may imagine that there were frequent gatherings and many heated discussions among the artistic confraternity, who were wont to meet in the shop of Baccio d'Agnolo; and it may have been in one of these discussions that "Michelangelo declared to Perugino that his art was absurd and antiquated." "*Goffo nell' arte*" – a bungler in his art – that is the precise phrase quoted by Vasari, and which so rankled in the breast of the elder man that, "Pietro being unable to support such an insult, they both carried their plaint before the magistracy of the Eight; in the which affair Pietro remained with but little credit."

It would have been better, we feel, and more dignified, to have passed over the slighting word with the contempt which it deserved. The master of the Sistine fresco which we have described, of the Albani altar-piece and its younger sister of the Certosa, of the altar-piece of the Magistrates' Chapel at Perugia, and the superb frescoes of the Cambio, stood far above such criticism in his own or any later age; and this appreciation of the Perugian's work in art does not imply any depreciation of Buonarroti's genius, of which, in its own sublime and individual path, the present writer is an enthusiastic admirer.

But Pietro was a strong-tempered and revengeful man, as is shown by the earlier records of Florentine justice, when he had appeared (in July of 1487) before the Eight – the "*Otto di Custodia*" – for having, with a notorious ruffian, one Aulista di Angelo of Perugia, waylaid a private enemy more than once with the intention of beating him – "*pluries et pluries nocturno tempore accesserunt armati quibusdam bastonibus.*" On that occasion he had escaped with a fine of ten florins of gold; and this later appearance does not seem, in its issue, to have been to the master's credit.

There was, besides this, much of truth in Buonarroti's criticism – a truth which added to the sting – that by this time Pietro's art had already begun to show old motives carelessly repeated. "Pietro," says our Vasari, "had worked so much, and had always such abundance of work in hand, that he often put the same things into his works; and had so reduced his art to a system that he gave to all his figures the same appearance." If this tendency appears even in his work before 1500, it becomes much more apparent later on; but to dwell on this point here would carry me too far, and for the present we are concerned with the master in his full strength at the date just mentioned. For the year 1500 dates the completion of the Cambio frescoes, and may be taken roughly as the great central date in Pietro's art. Before describing in detail those frescoes, let us consider what other commissions had preceded that of the Perugian bankers.

Foremost among these must come the great altar-piece of the Certosa of Pavia, to which I have frequently alluded. It had been commissioned by Duke Lodovico Sforza of Milan soon after the artist left Venice – the great Certosa monastery being always under the personal patronage of the Dukes of Milan. Pietro seems to have been working at it already in 1496, and it was completed, on the Duke's pressing instance, by the end of 1499. It has only remained partially in its original place – in the second chapel on the left of the great Carthusian church. The upper central painting – that of the Eternal Father – is still by Perugino, the three lower panels are copies from the originals, now in the National Gallery of London, and the panels at the side are by Borgognone.

Nothing that the master of Perugia has left us exceeds in tranquil beauty these central panels of the London National Gallery. Orsini tells us that from 1795 the Certosa painting with its six panels had passed into the possession of the ducal family of Melzi at Milan; but this is not quite correct, for we have seen that the panel of the Eternal Father is still in place. In 1856 Duke Melzi parted with his three panels to the London Gallery. In the centre panel the sweet, pensive Virgin is adoring the child Jesus, who is watched over by an angel, as in Leonardo's famous "Madonna of the Rocks," while three angels make music in the sky above; on the right of this is the Archangel Raphael with the young Tobias; on the left the lovely figure of the Archangel Michael, fully armed, with legs apart set firmly on the ground, and left hand resting on his shield – a figure which the master repeated more than once, notably in the great Assumption of the Virgin in the Florence Academy.

Perugino was married at this time to the beautiful Chiara

Fancelli, and there is little doubt that she appears in more than one of his pictures; in particular, she is said to have posed for the Archangel Raphael of this Certosa altar-piece. Next to the beauty of type in this and other figures, we have to notice the pure rich colouring and the extraordinary beauty, in the central panel, of the landscape background. All the Umbrian sense of space is there, in this valley with its winding stream and blue distances, while in the middle distance the delicately drawn trees are mirrored against the clear sky. It is a picture one would love to live with, and, without possessing the rapt devotion, the deep inner spirit, which pervades the paintings of Angelico, its atmosphere is calm, restful, and in that sense prayerful.

A whole group of other paintings, attractive and interesting, though of lesser interest, belongs to this splendidly fertile period of Pietro's genius. The Fano altar-piece – a Virgin and Child with Saints – dates from a visit in 1497, and an Annunciation followed in the next year, while at Sinigaglia and Cantiano there are very similar works. Both the Fano pictures, which I have not seen, have been carefully described by Dr. Williamson in his monograph on this artist. The Madonna Crowned, with the Child on her knee and a group of kneeling penitents behind, now in the Perugian Gallery, was painted for the confraternity of San Pietro Martire in 1497; and there is in the same gallery a somewhat similar work, painted for another confraternity, with two saints (one of whom is St. Bernardino) kneeling in the foreground, and in the distance Perugia, with the yet untouched towers of the Baglioni.

To the same period have been attributed the Family of St. Anne, at Marseilles, and the Virgin in Glory, of the Bologna Gallery, with its armed St. Michael and its lovely female figure of St. Apollonia; and now we come to a creation which, in its fine drawing and composition and its atmosphere of tranquil beauty, takes a place beside the Certosa altar-piece or that of the Perugian Magistrates' Chapel. I refer to the Virgin appearing to St. Bernard, now in the Munich Gallery. The theme was a favourite one at this period of Italian art, for it has been treated with great beauty by Filippino Lippi in his painting in the Badia at Florence. The Munich picture was destined by our master for S. Spirito at Florence, and was acquired (in 1829) by King Ludwig of Bavaria from the Capponi family, who held the rights over the chapel where it hung. As in Filippino's rendering, the monastic saint is seated in study or adoration, and looks up, with a startled gesture, to see the Virgin enter with a train of lovely angels; but what Filippino fails to equal – even with his delicious angels, who might be taken from Florentine urchins – is the sense of tranquil beauty which comes to us in these figures of the Perugian master, and is continued in that wonderful sweep of distant landscape seen through the open colonnade. A study for this fine painting is among the drawings in the Uffizi Gallery.

I have already had occasion to mention the great Crucifixion of S. Maria Maddalena de' Pazzi (completed 1496), and a very similar treatment of this subject appears in a later Crucifixion painted for the Convent of S. Jerome in Florence, and now in the Accademia of that city. Here, in the three figures introduced, the Christ and the Virgin mother are almost reproduced from those in the larger fresco of S. Maria Maddalena, but are coarser and more careless in the painting. The city here in the distance has been traced to be Florence, and the date suggested is about 1498. Closer yet to this central date of the Perugian master's work is the great Vallombrosa "Assumption" (dated 1500); but this very probably succeeded immediately in order of time to the Sala del Cambio frescoes, and therefore I leave it for the moment to speak of the earlier, but most important, commission of the altar-piece of the Magistrates' Chapel at Perugia. A painting to decorate this chapel, and which was to include the portraits of the Priori, the governing body then in office, had been commissioned from Pietro as early as 1483, and the contract actually signed; but the master had more important work on hand – notably his frescoes for the chapel of Pope Sixtus – and it was not till twelve years later, in 1495, that, being again in Perugia and at the summit of his fame, he was successfully captured by the magistrates of that city, and signed a fresh contract on far higher terms (one hundred golden ducats, but with a time limit of six months for the work) to paint the altar-piece of their chapel. The result was the masterpiece which now hangs in the Vatican Gallery, and shows us the Virgin enthroned with the Child standing upright on her knee, beneath such an open portico as appears in the "Vision of St. Bernard," and with beside her four grave attendant saints, as robed and mitred bishops. Here the master varies a little his frequent signature – for *Petrus de Chastro Plebis pinxit* gives as his birthplace the little Umbrian city of Città della Pieve.

The great altar-piece, which possesses all the devotional beauty and repose of his best period, was this time completed within the time agreed, and took its honoured place within the Magistrates' Chapel at Perugia, whence it was torn away by the invading French in 1797, and found its way back, not to Perugia, but to the Vatican collection at Rome. Perugia, especially in the person of her greatest master, Pietro Vannucci, suffered terribly at the hands of Napoleon; and here I must express my appreciation of the able description given by my friend Dr. G. C. Williamson of what he very aptly calls "the story of the pillage."

Perugia in 1796 was very rich in the works of her master, Pietro Perugino. "Almost every church possessed pictures by the master. The altar-piece painted in 1495 for the Magistrates' Chapel was still *in situ*, and public buildings were full of rich decoration." But Napoleon, a man whose life was steeped in battle and human bloodshed, seems by a strange contrast to have had a particular fancy for the quiet devotional art of the Umbrian master. His commissioner, one Tinet by name, had orders to ransack Perugia, and six cartloads of her treasured paintings, drawn by oxen, left the city for Paris. One altar-piece, that of the Magistrates' Chapel, was nearly forgotten, but remembered at the last moment, and included. But even so, the terrible conqueror who held Italy beneath his feet was not contented, and a fresh decree, of 1811, ordered more pictures to be sent for his Paris collection. A certain

Tofanelli was now the agent for further spoliation, and by diligent search forty-eight more pictures were squeezed out of unlucky Perugia, and in November of 1813 forwarded, viâ Rome, to Paris. Napoleon had now more works of Perugino than he could find place for in his gallery of the Louvre, and gave many of them away to the provincial museums of France; and thus it happens that the works of our master are distributed, in fragmentary condition in panels from his famous altar-pieces, among the French provincial cities – such towns as Bordeaux, Marseilles, Lyons, Grenoble, Nantes, Rouen, and Caen, where they are practically inaccessible to the average student – while only a small portion of the once rich collection of his works remains within the Perugian Pinacoteca.

But fortunately his masterpiece in fresco painting within the Sala del Cambio could not be so easily torn from the walls. I have already alluded to the acceptance by the master in 1499 of this commission, for which he had refused the decoration of Orvieto Duomo. The actual space offered him to decorate by the Perugian bankers in their Sala del Cambio was not very great, but the result was a thing of perfect beauty – "a little gem" (I called it in my notes written at Perugia, and published some years ago) "of decorative Renaissance art. It is a small room, panelled with the loveliest tarsia work (this too from Vannucci's design), and above these panels the master's frescoes. The 'Nativity' and 'Trans-figuration' at the end of the room are among his finest, ripest works, and on each side are the Prophets and Sibyls, or heroes, kings, and sages of antiquity – Leonidas the Spartan, Trajan the wise Roman emperor, Fabius 'Cunctator,' Socrates, Horatius, who kept the bridge, and the Roman Camillus."

It is most probable that the whole scheme of decoration, and of these classic sages and heroes in particular, with their guiding virtues above, was supplied to the artist by the humanist Maturanzio, Secretary to the "Priori" of Perugia, and acting under their orders; while Maturanzio himself may have drawn his inspiration from a MS. Cicero in the Perugian Library, in whose miniatures the four cardinal virtues appear beside the heroes who displayed them in their lives. Such a dictation was quite in the traditions of the best Italian art. I have shown in an earlier work – "The Renaissance in Italian Art" – how this was probably the case in the famous frescoes of the Spanish chapel at Florence, where Ruskin had pictured the artist himself as giving his message of religious dogmatic teaching to the world; and later we shall see how the Marchioness of Mantua, Isabella d'Este, ties down our Pietro most mercilessly in the allegorical painting which she commissions.

But here, in the rendering at least, Perugino is entirely himself, and all these figures, whether heroes of heathendom or sages or prophets – Isaiah, Moses, David, and Daniel – or virtues or lovely sibyls, are painted in one key of tranquil, devotional beauty. "Obliged," says Addington Symonds, "to treat in the Sala del Cambio the representative heroes of Greek and Roman story, he adopted the manner of his religious paintings. Leonidas, the lion-hearted Spartan, and Cato, the austere Roman, bend their mild heads like flowers in Perugino's frescoes, and gather up their drapery in studied folds with celestial delicacy."

In the ceiling, which, if not painted by himself, is undoubtedly from his design, he had perhaps a freer hand in the arrangement, and has created a very lovely piece of decoration. Here the deities of the old heathen world appear as imaged in that delicious sentiment of the earlier Renaissance. Venus is wafted through the sky, drawn by two doves; Luna, nude to the waist, sits in a chariot with her nymphs in harness; Mercury holds his *caduceus*, the serpent wand; Apollo drives his four-horsed chariot; and – loveliest group of all – Jupiter receives the cup of nectar from young Ganymede, "such a cup-bearer" (I wrote in my Perugian notes) "as the tyrants of the Visconti or the Baglioni may have had – a slim young page with long floating curls, his limbs clad in tight red hose, and long ribbons twining around him, as on bent knee he offers the cup to his master."

His fellow-citizens wished the master to include his own

portrait in the frescoes of their Cambio, and here it is, for us, a square, solid-looking face of middle life, whose hair escapes from the tight red cap – a face not perhaps attractive, but of intellect-uality and power, and with great determination in the lines of mouth and chin. The Latin lines of compliment beneath are probably due to the scholarly pen of Maturanzio, and on the other side the words *Anno Salut. MD* give the date of the work's completion – the central date, as we may fairly take it, of Perugino's genius, and his life-work in art. It is the moment when he climbs the hill-top – this fateful year that divides the century – and stands upon the highest ground; henceforth for him too, as for his country, the slow years mark the footsteps of decline.

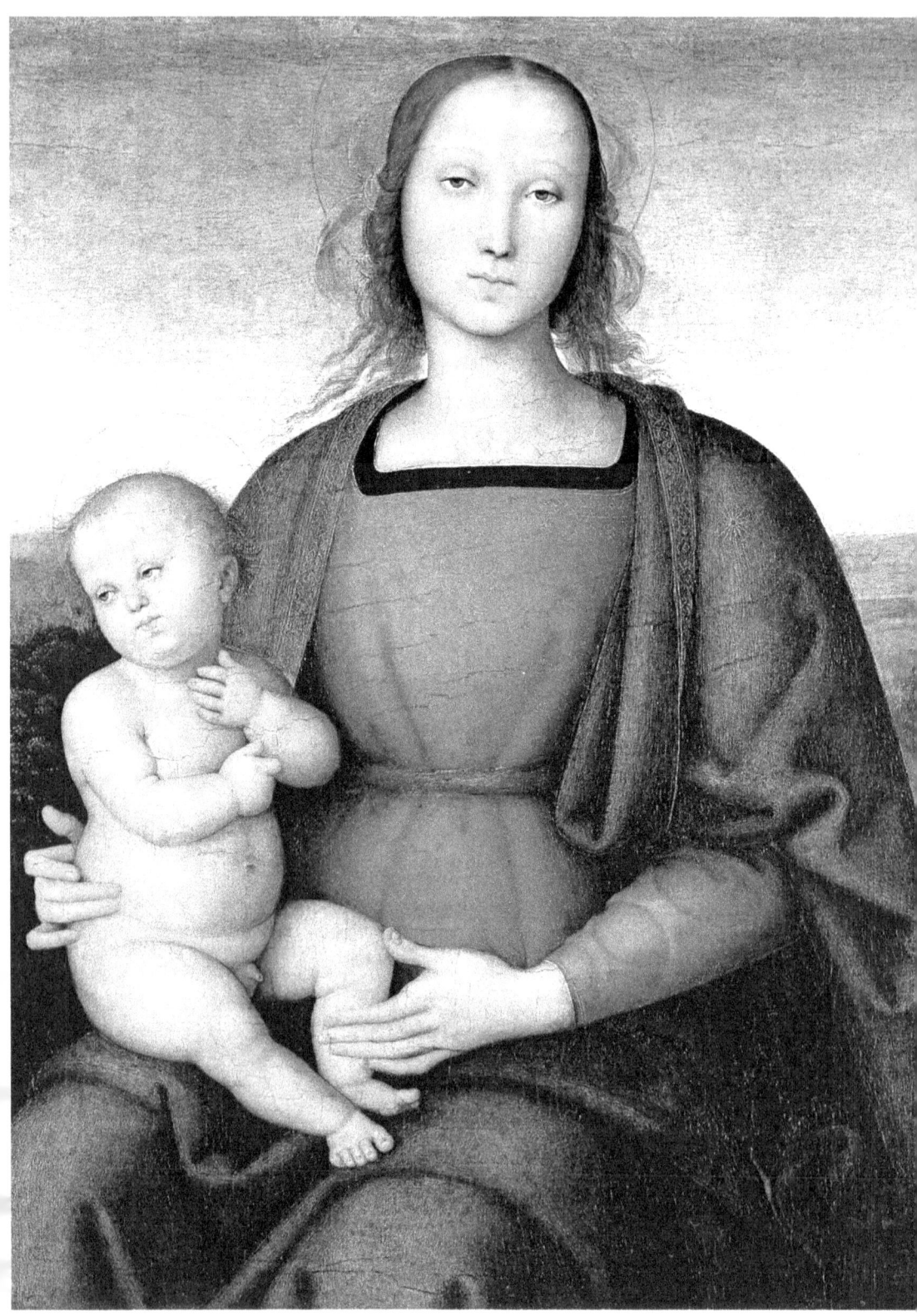

Perugino, Madonna and Child, 1500

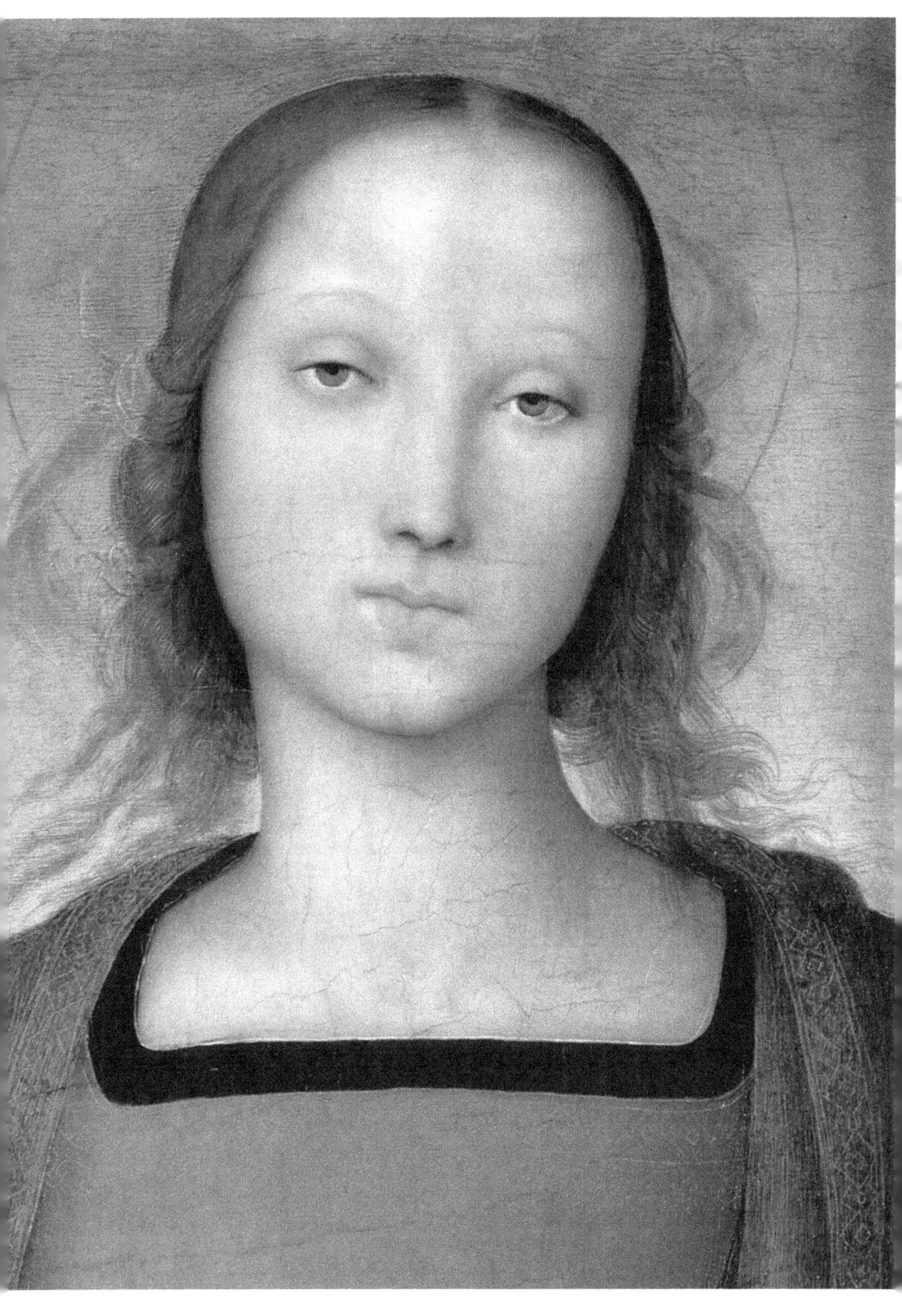

Perugino, Madonna and Child, 1500, detail

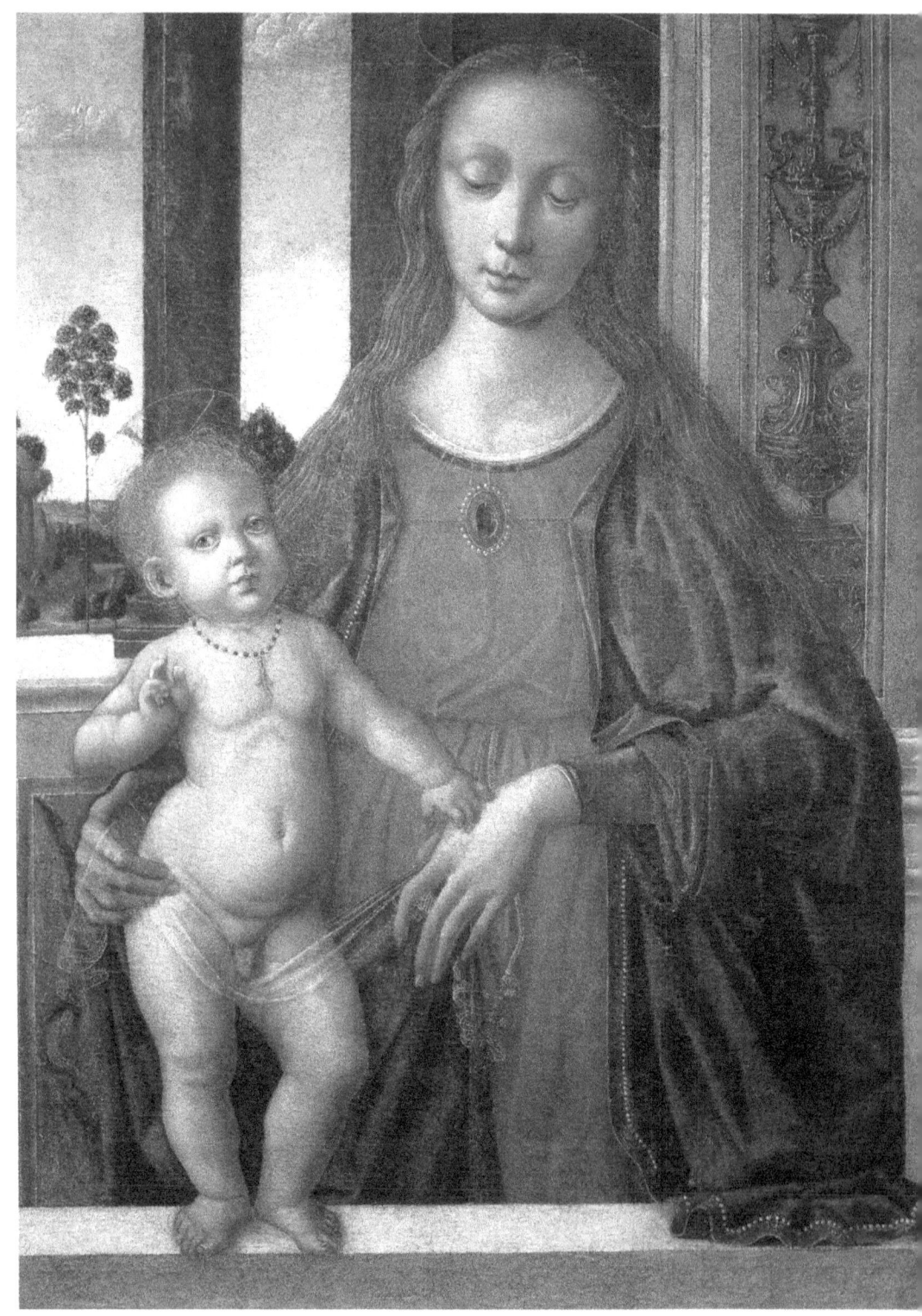

Perugino, Madonna and Child, 1470-73

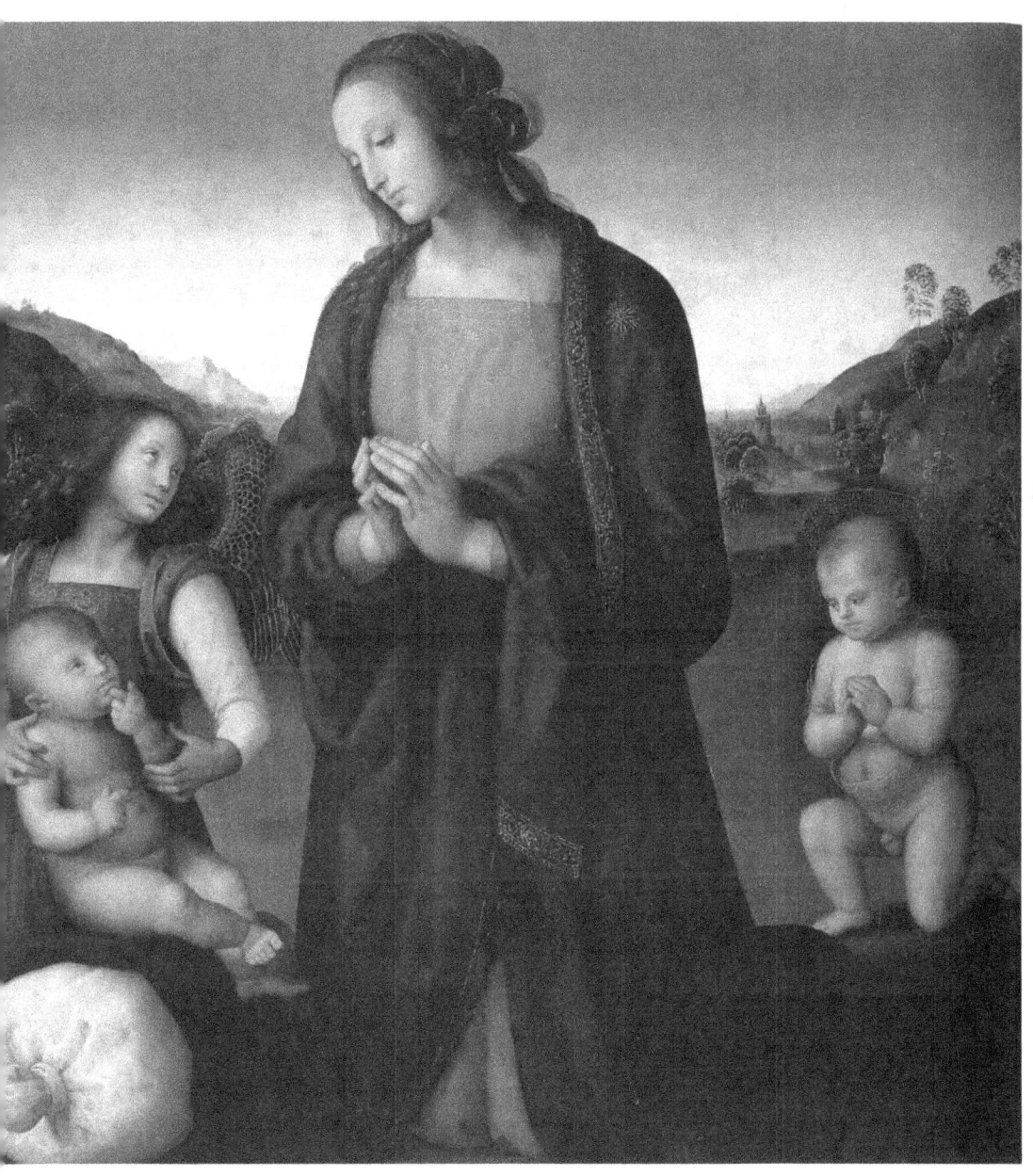

Perugino, Madonna and Child, 1445-48,
Pitti Palace

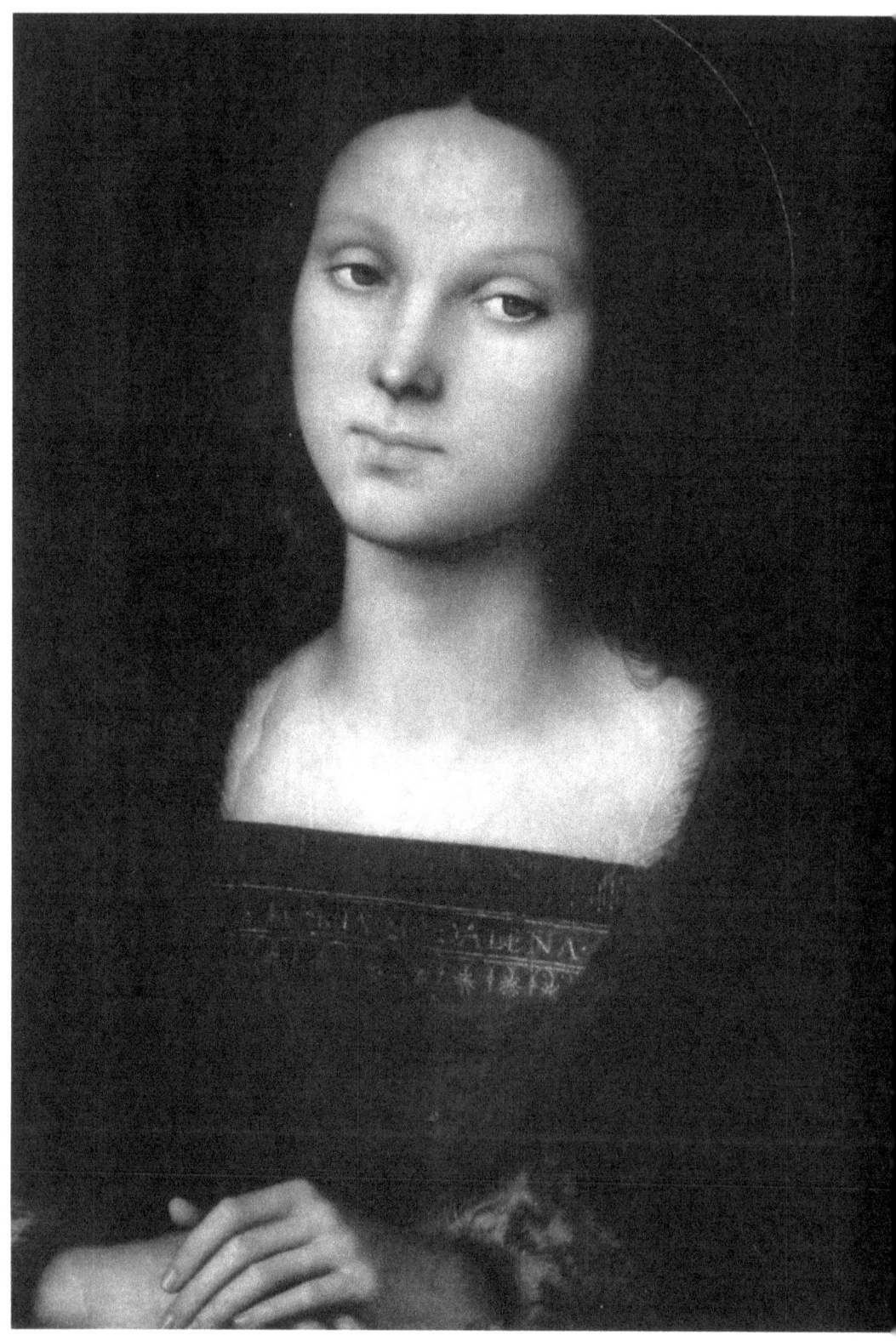

Perugino, Mary Magdalene, 1445-48

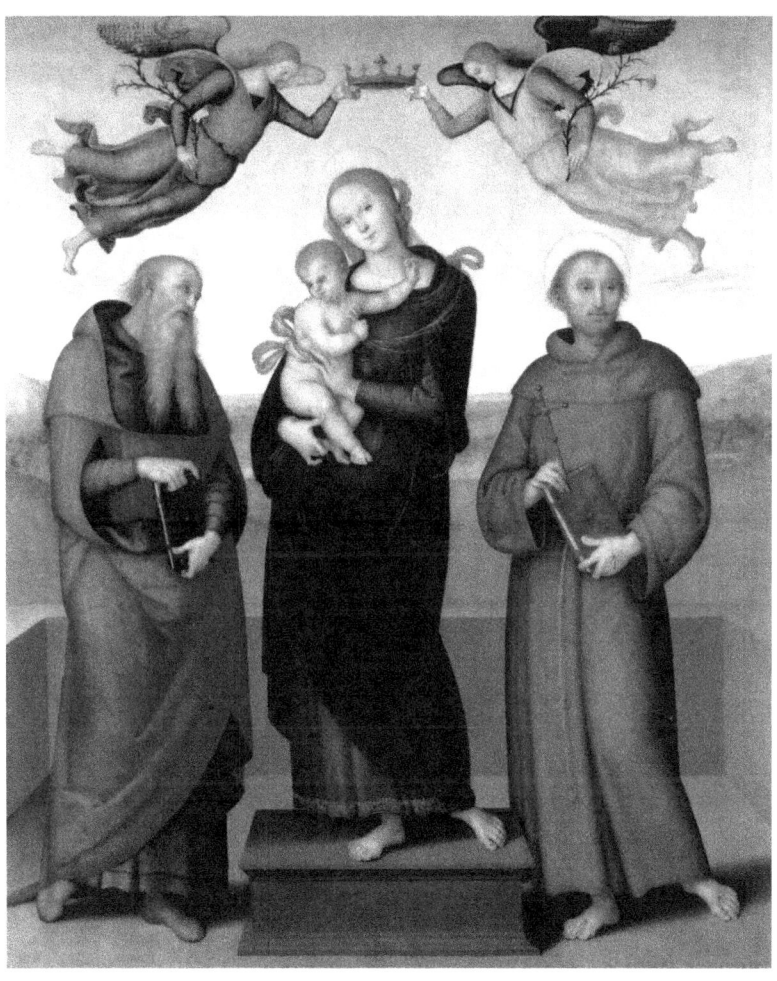

Perugino, Virgin and Child With Saints, 1507,
National Gallery, London

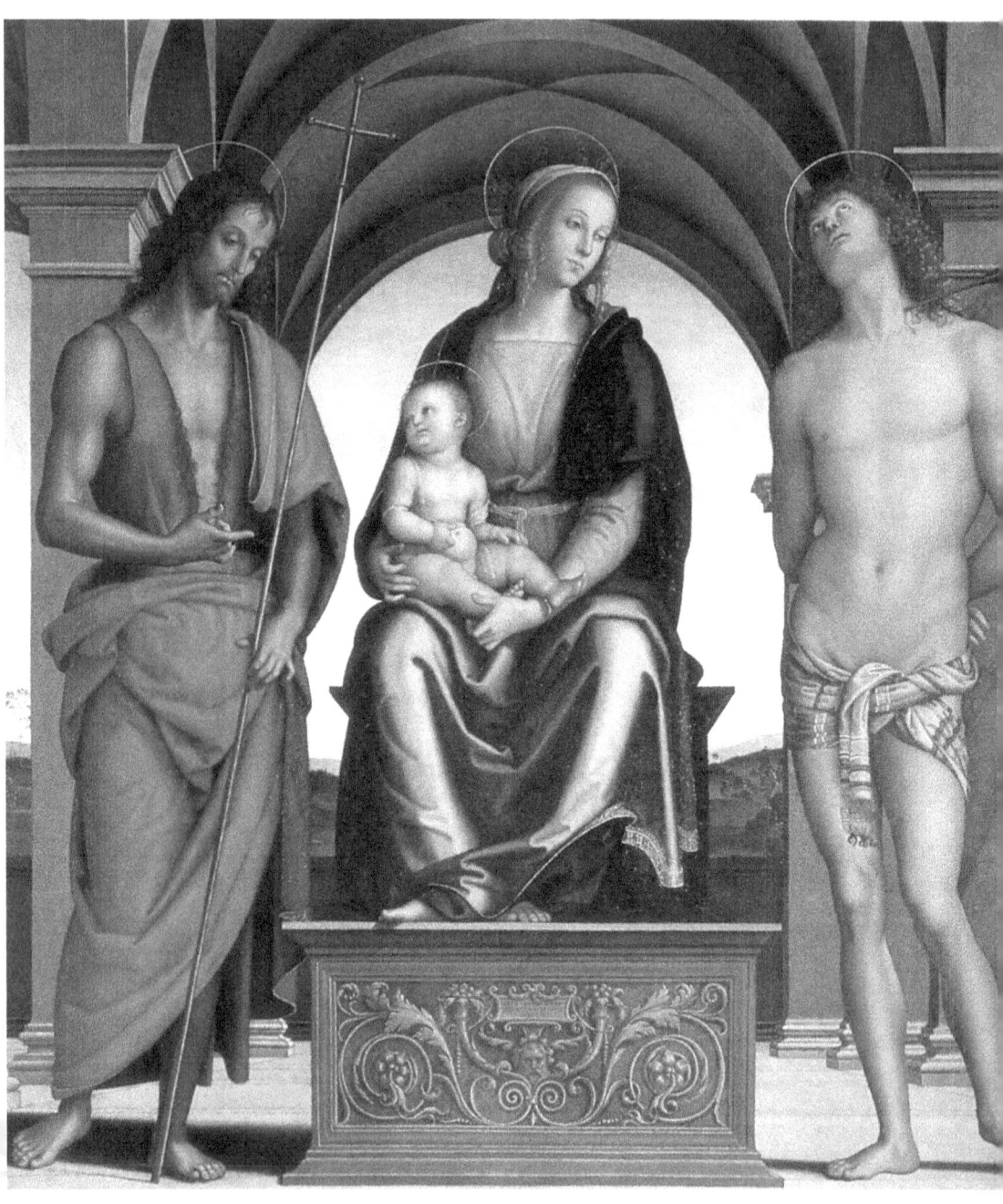

Perugino, The Madonna, Child and Saints,
1493, Uffizi

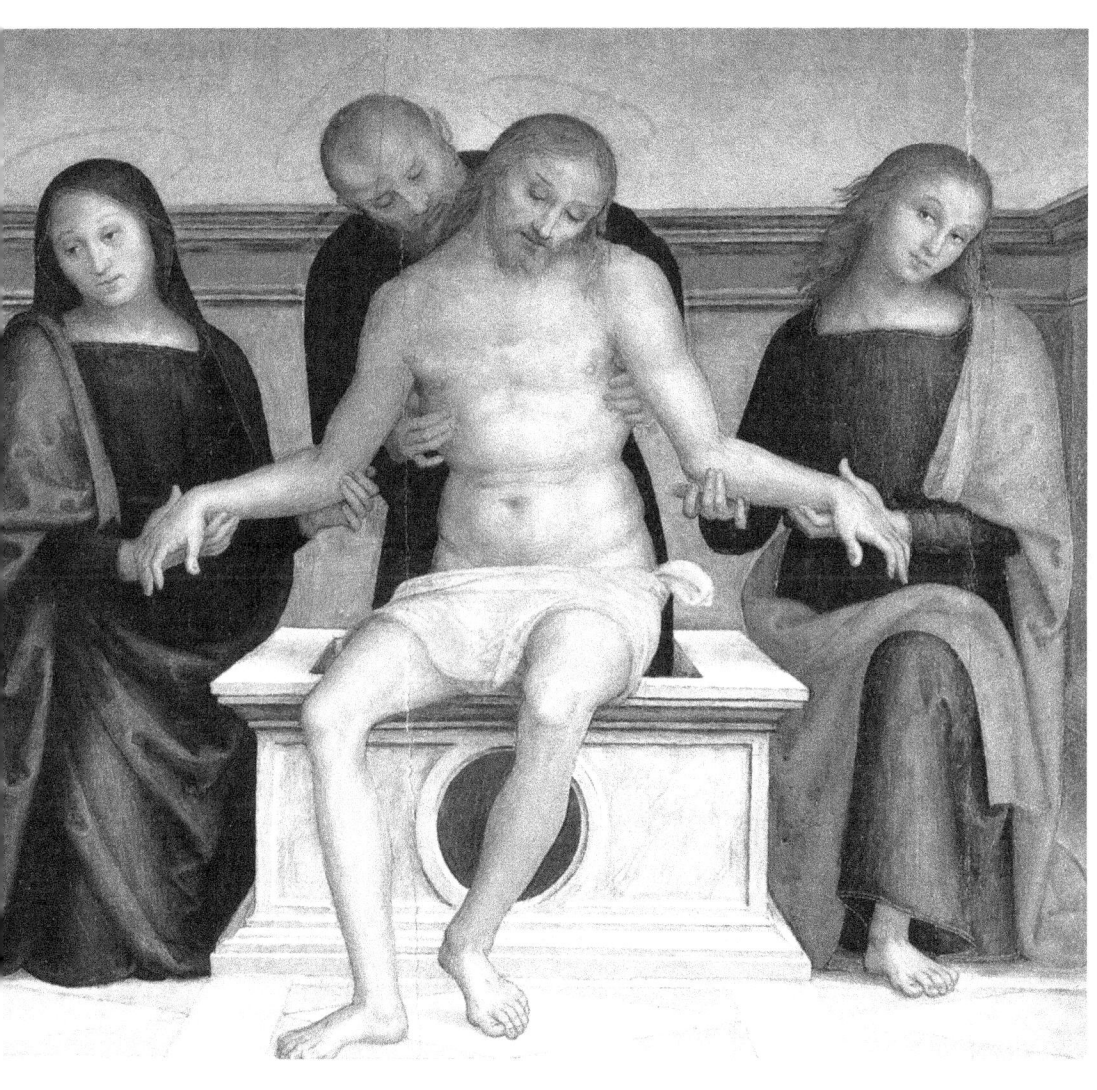

Perugino, The Dead Christ, 1512-13

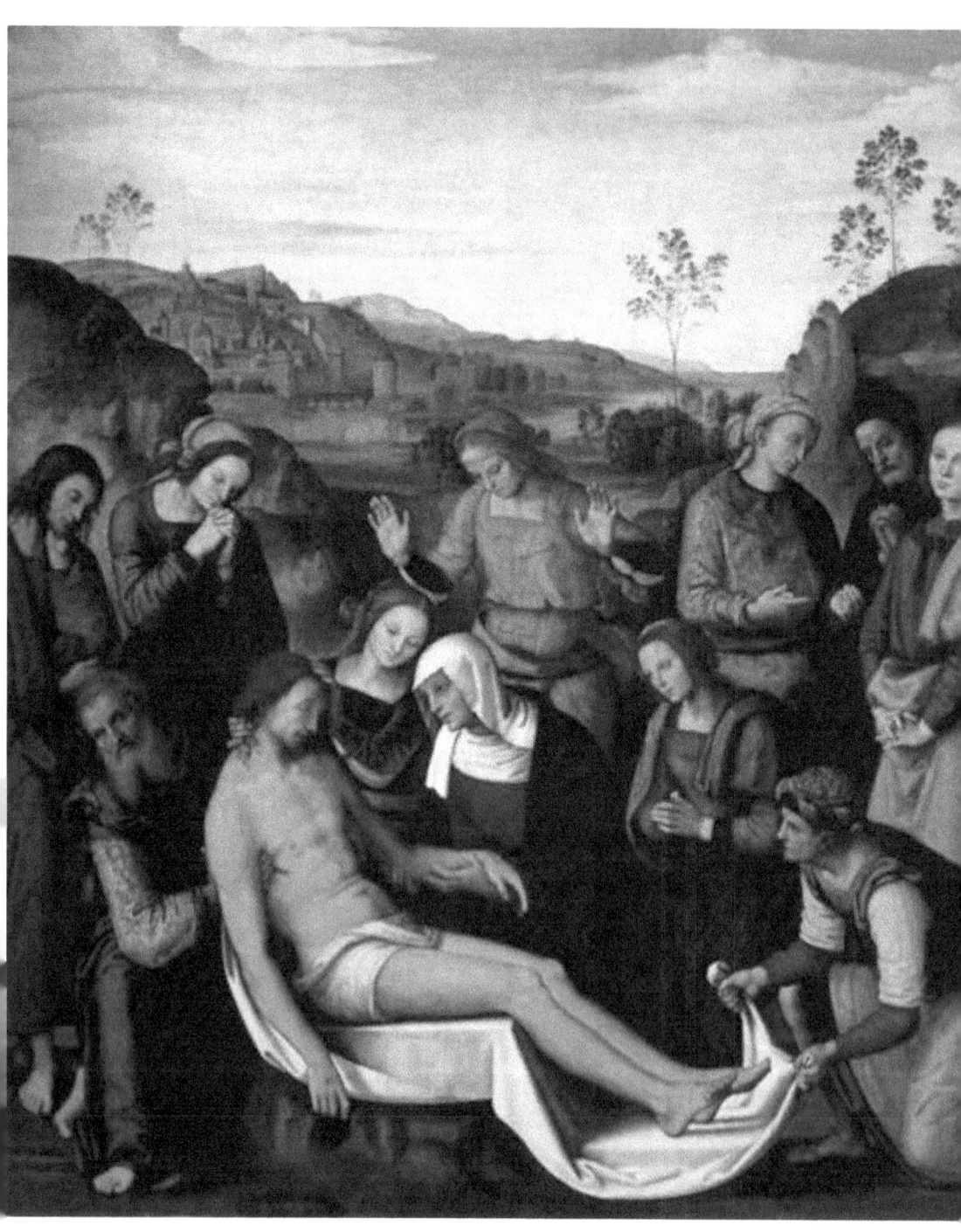

Perugino, The Mourning of the Dead Christ, 1495

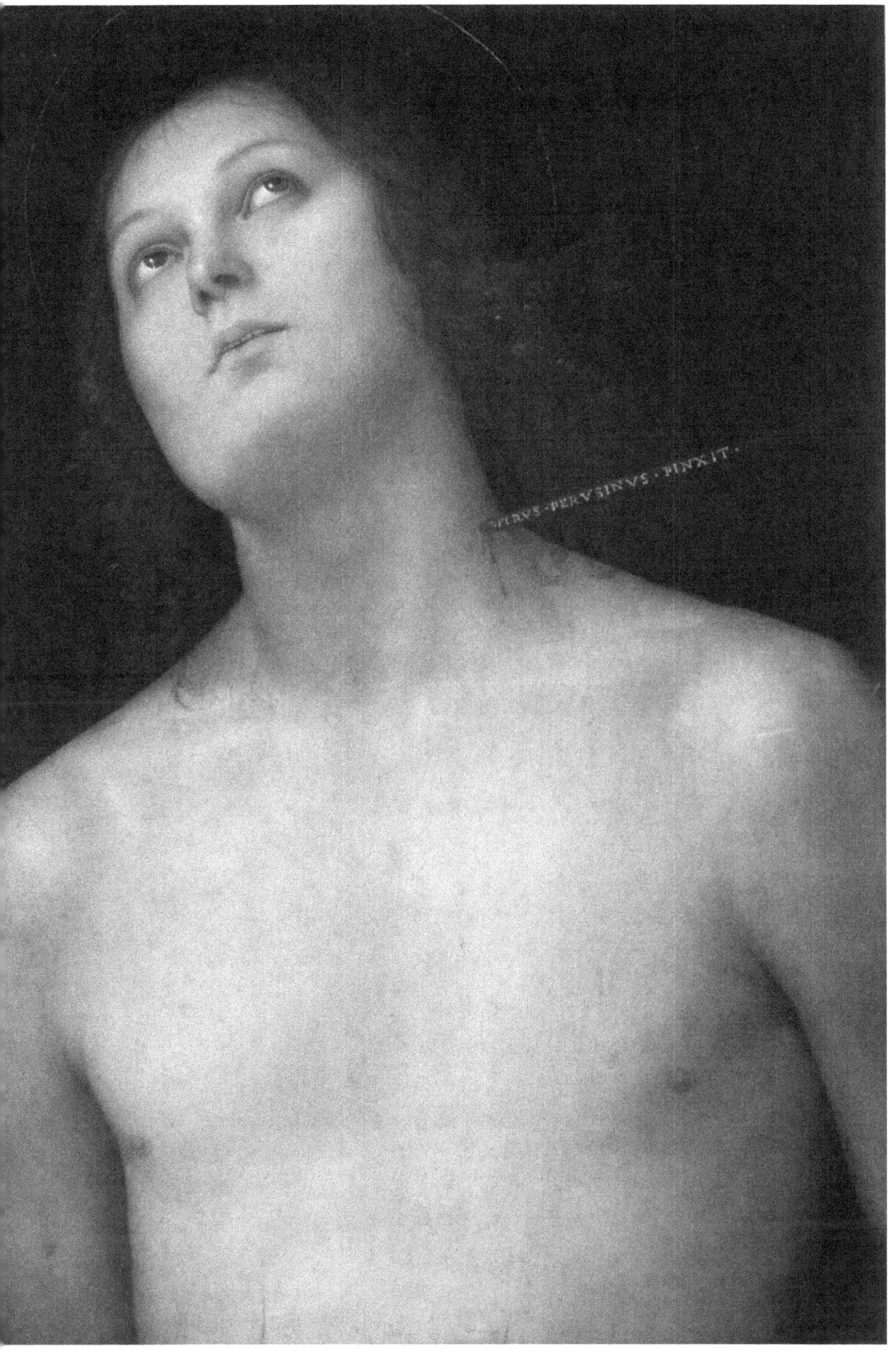

Perugino, St Sebastian, 1475-78

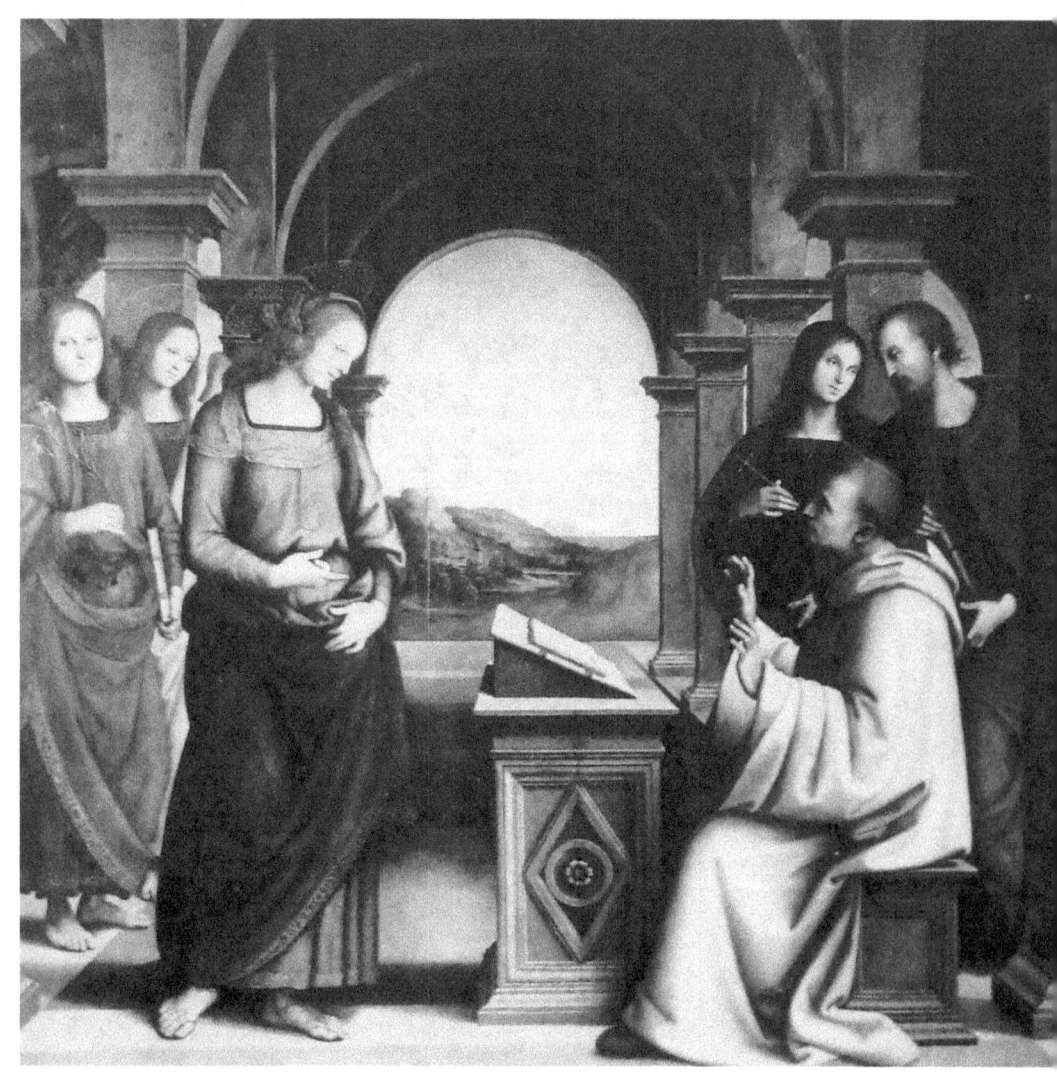

Perugino, Vision of St Bernard, 1488

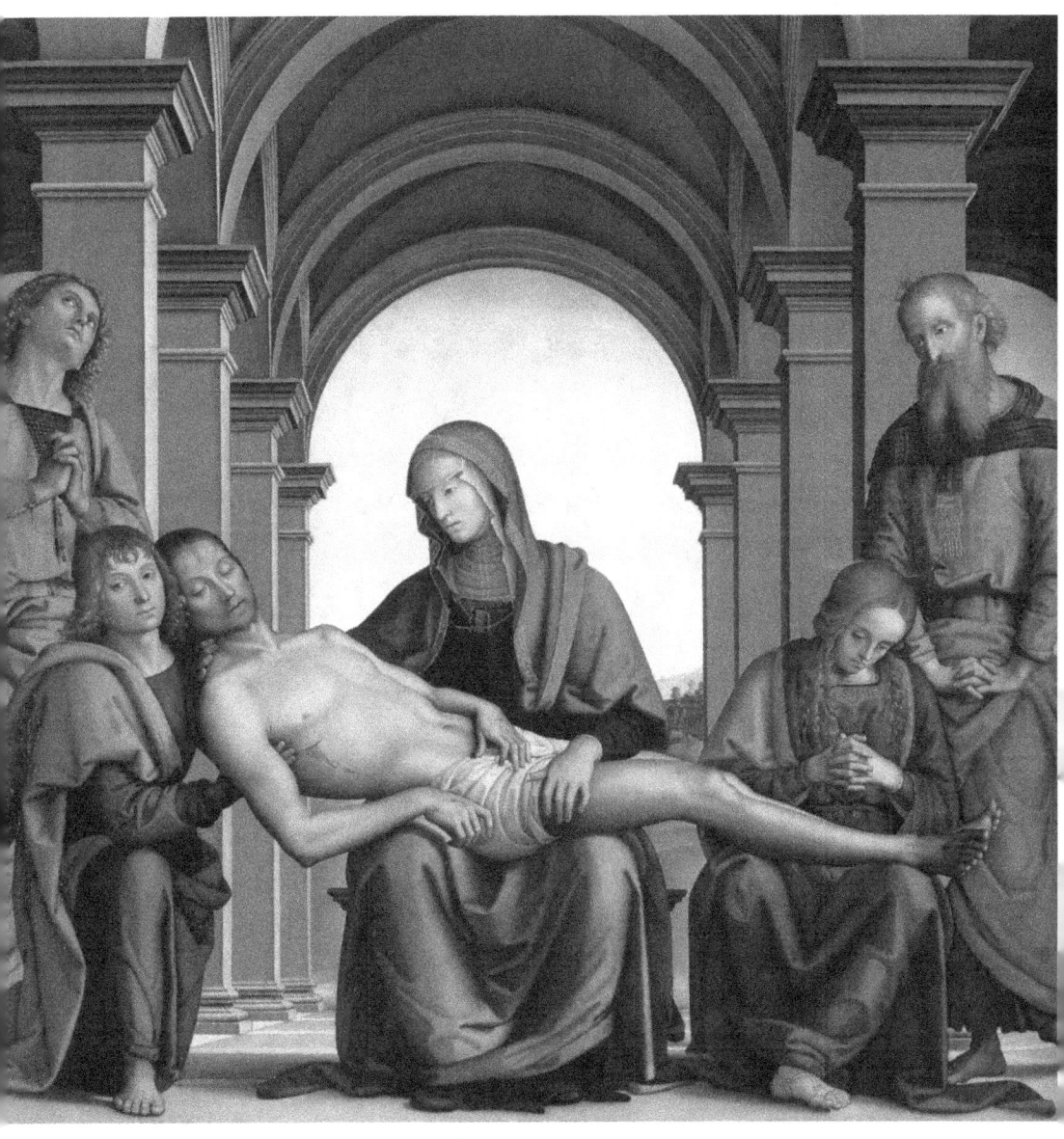

Perugino, Pietà, 1490, Uffizi

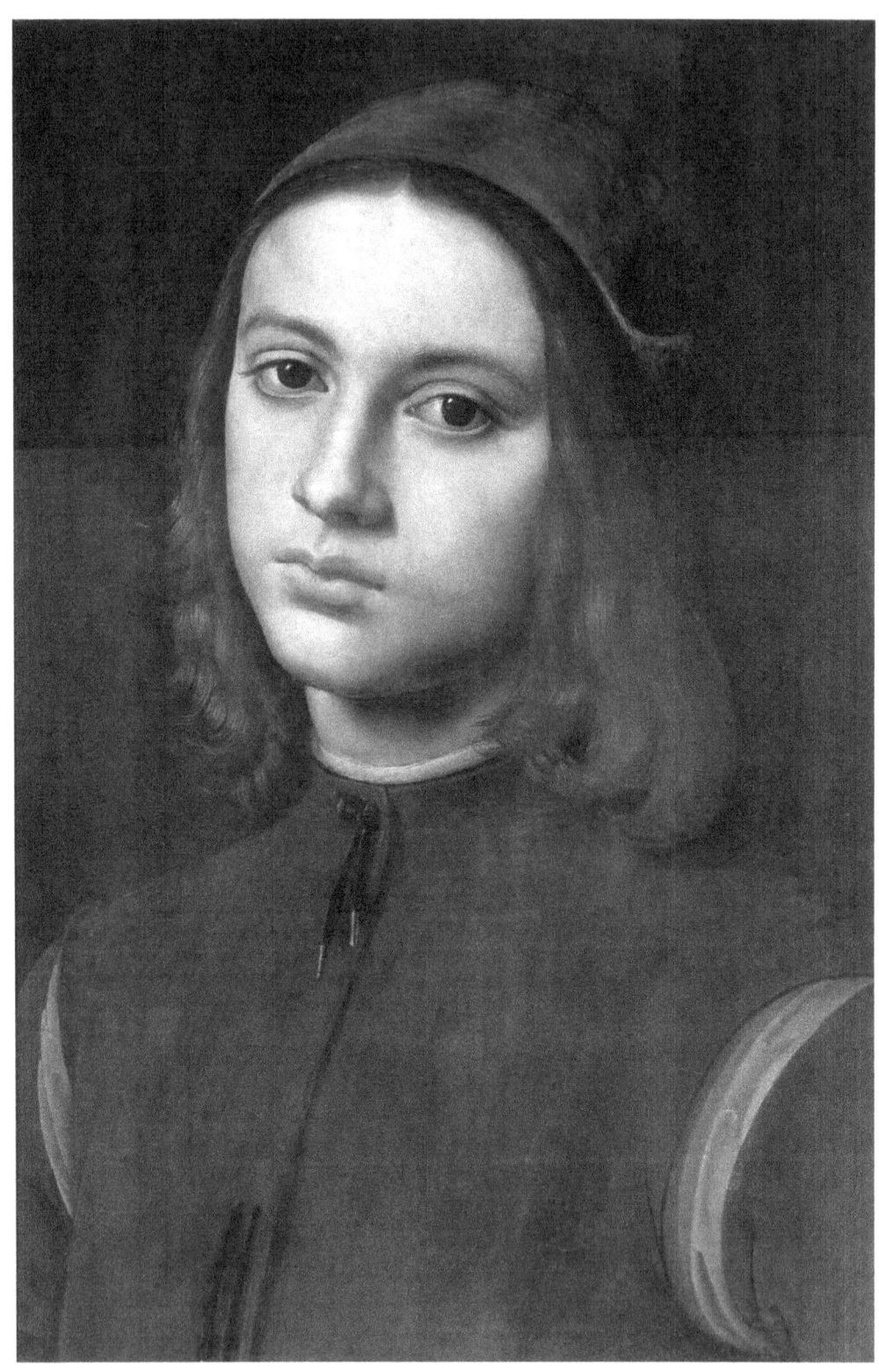

Perugino, possible Portrait of Alessandro Braccesi,
1480, Uffizi

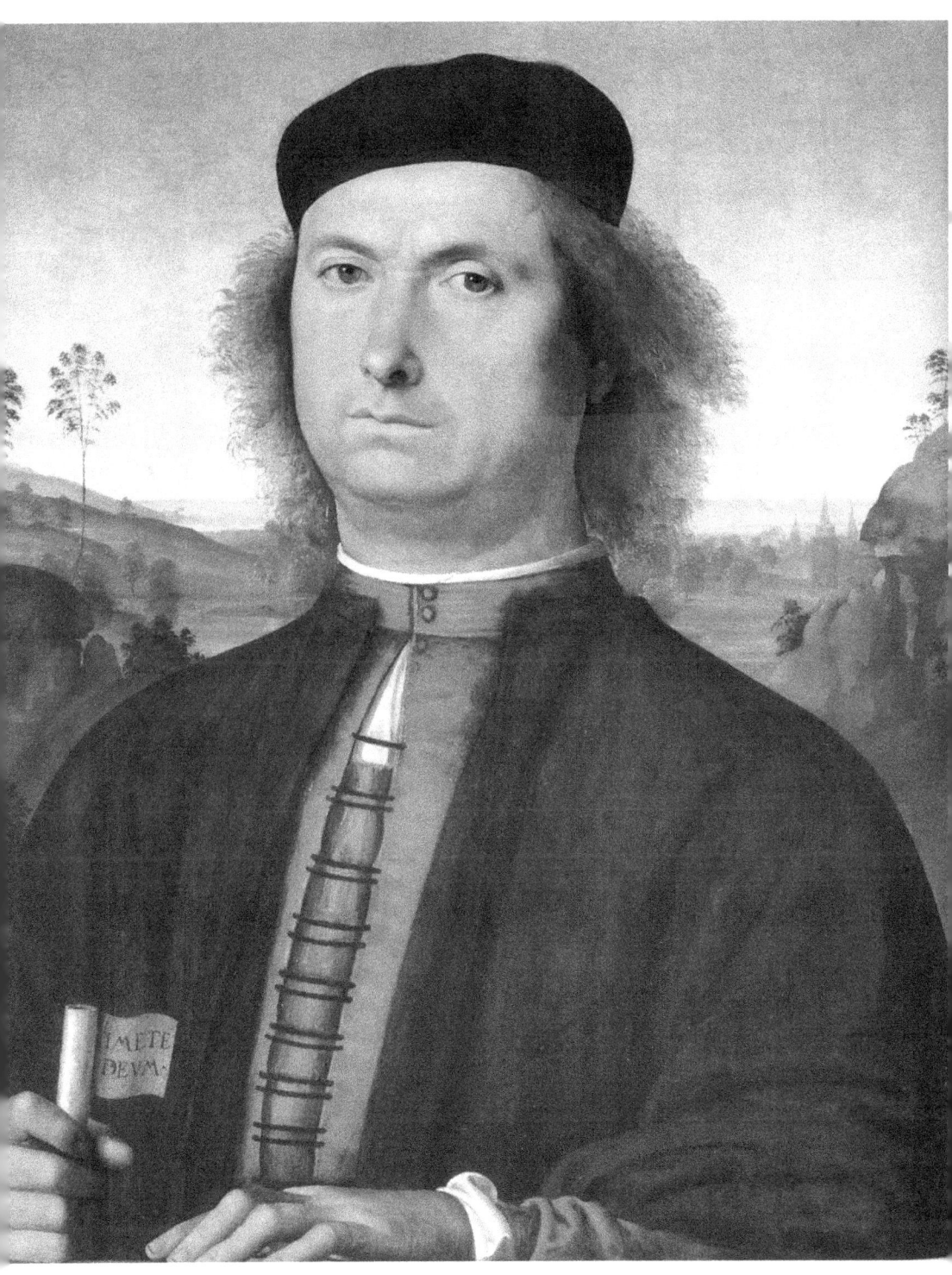

Perugino, Francesco delle Opere, 1494, Uffizi

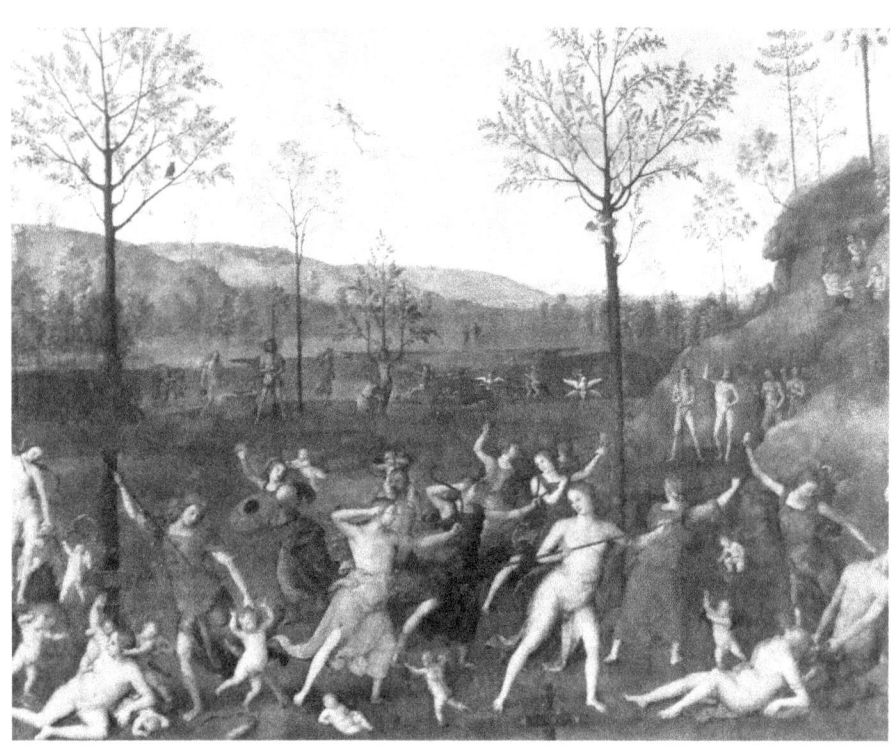

Perugino, The Battle of Love and Chastity, 1503-05

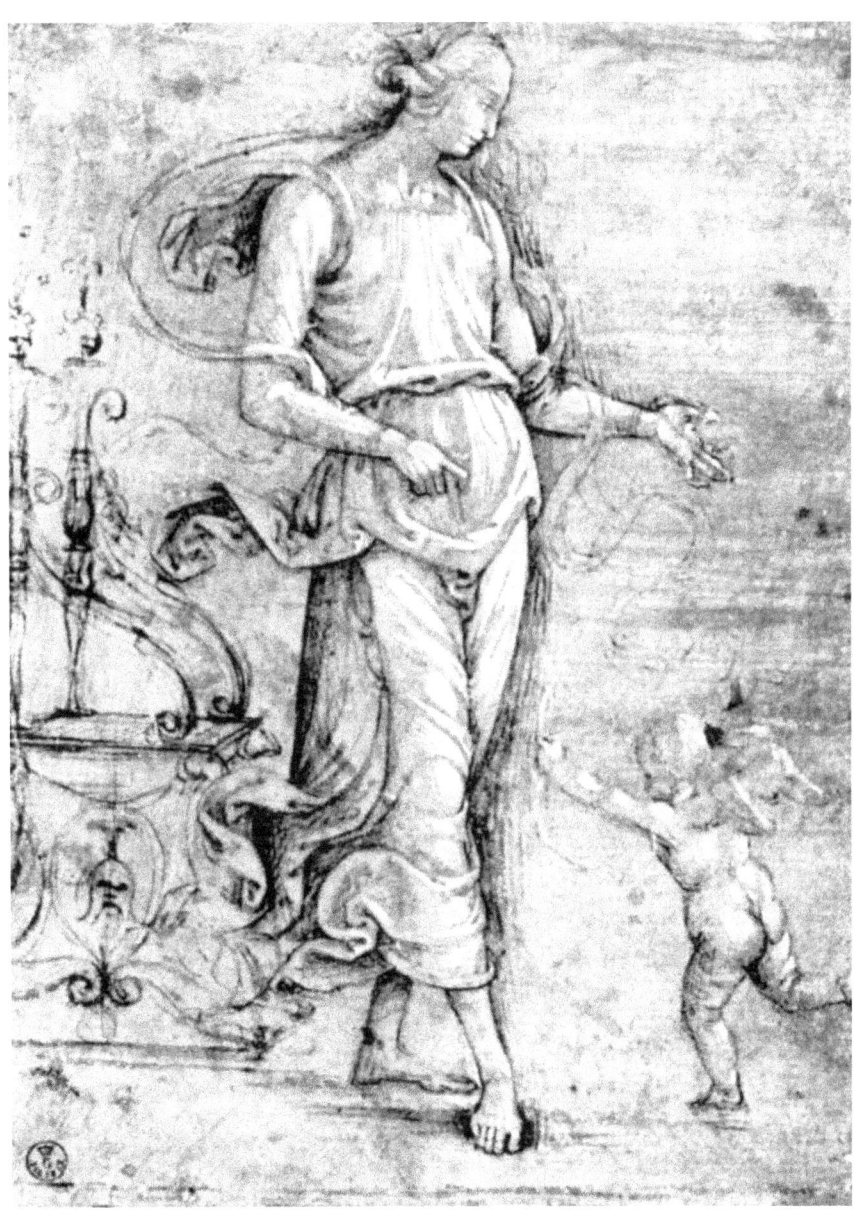

Perugino, Venus and Cupid, 1497-1500, Uffizi Gallery

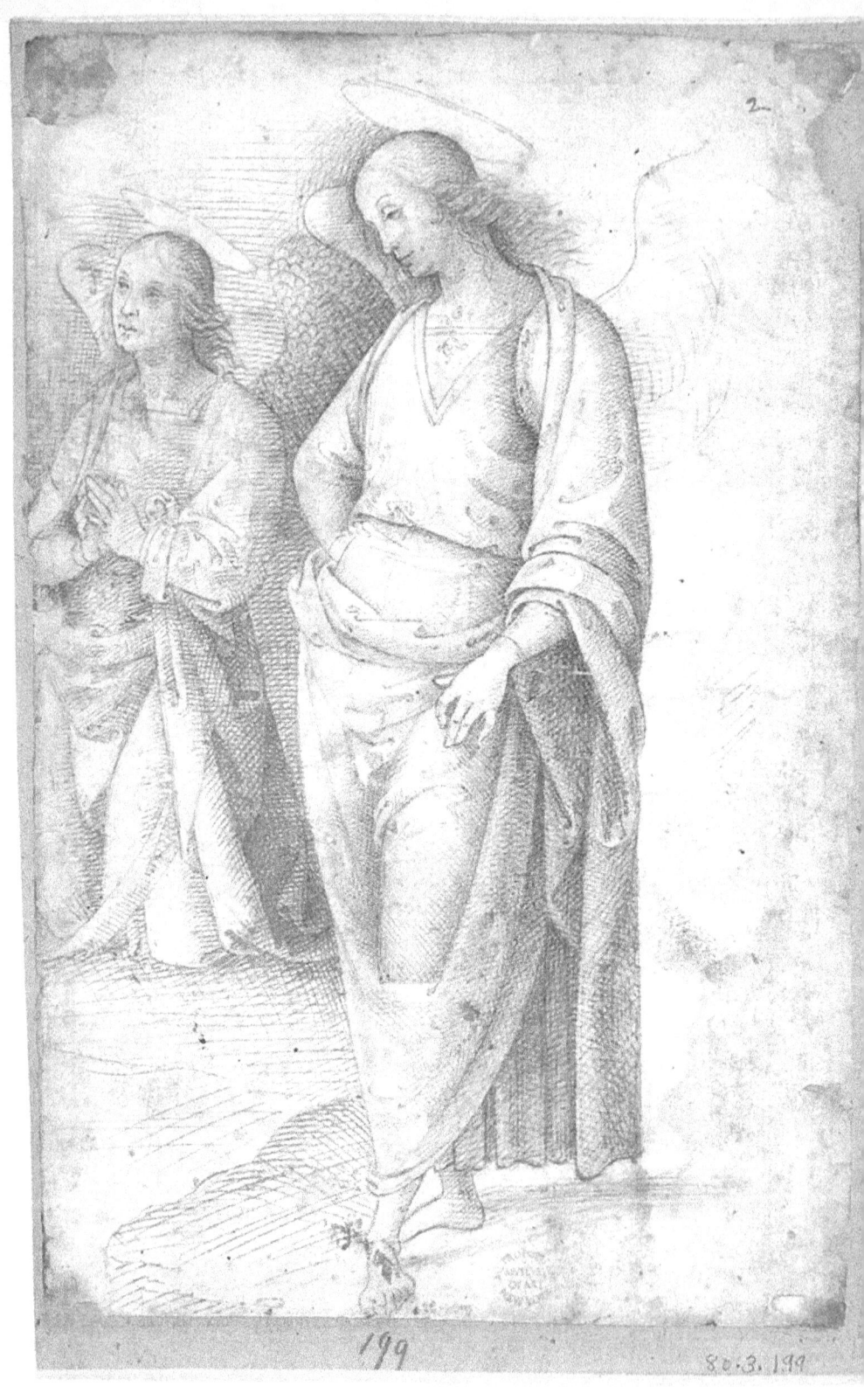

Perugino, Two Figures of Angels Standing,
Metropolitan Museum of Art, NYC

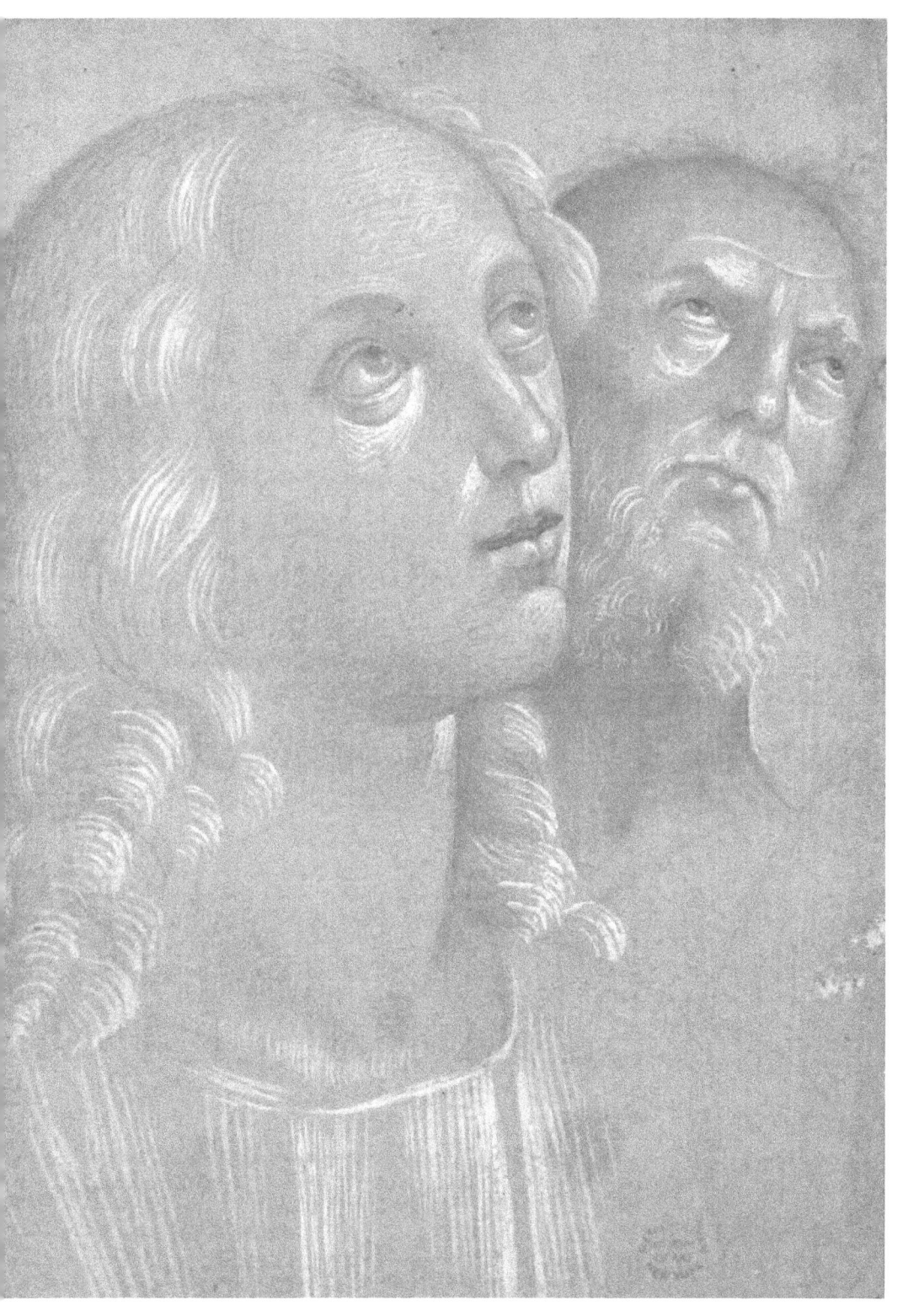

Perugino, Heads of Two Saints, Metropolitan Museum of Art, NYC

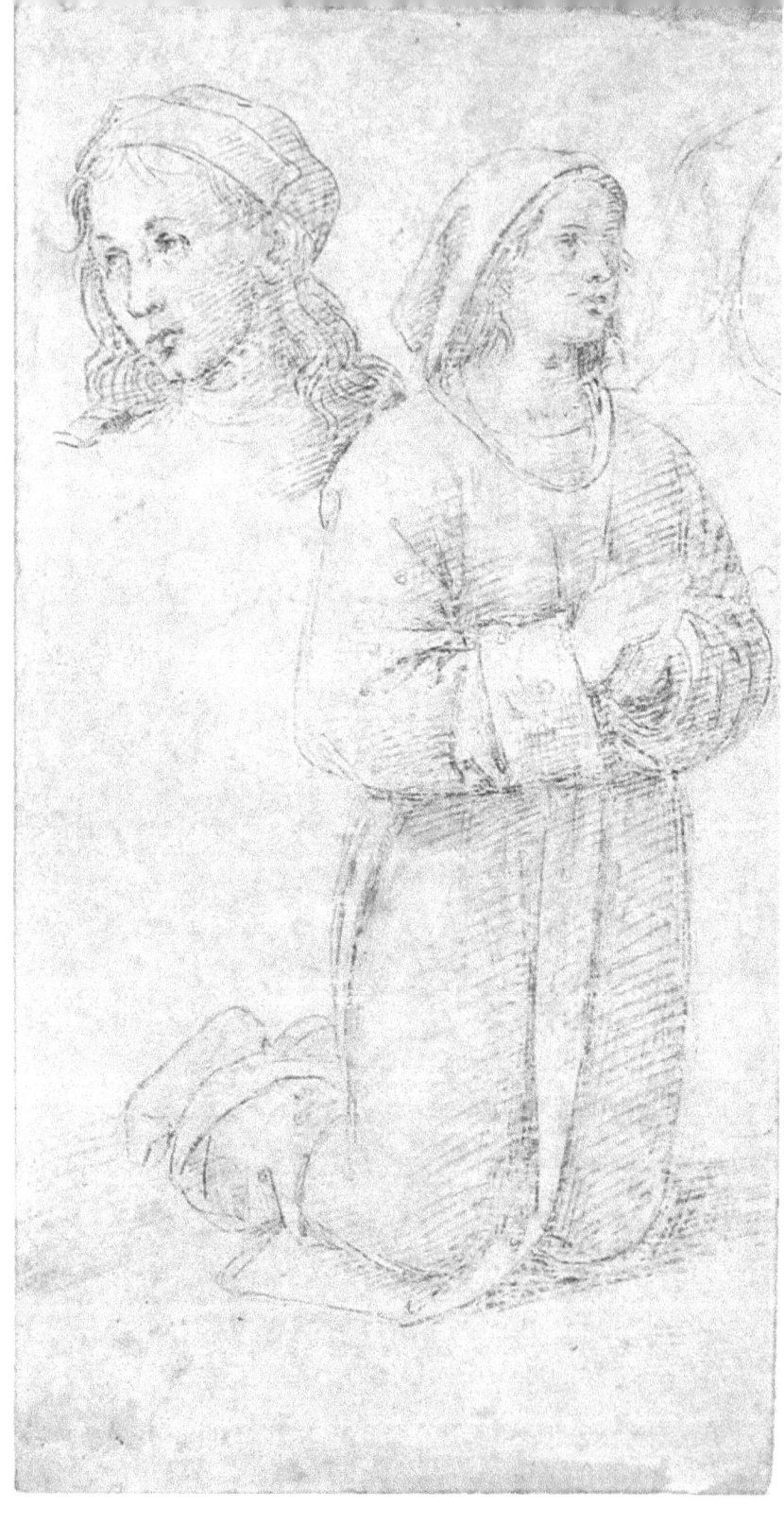

Perugino, Study of a Kneeling Youth,
and of the Head of Another, 1500, New York

III

Rafaelle Sanzio of Urbino had lost his mother, Magia Ciarla, in 1491, and his father, Giovanni Santi, three years later. It was not long after this that he was placed by his relatives for instruction in Perugino's famous workshop at Perugia, and we may safely assume that he was there during part of the master's richly creative period which we have just traversed, and that his hand was busied, along with those of other pupils, in the paintings of the frescoes of the Sala del Cambio.

Among these pupils Vasari mentions, beside Rafaelle, the Florentines – Rocco Zoppo, Baccio, and Francesco Ubertino (the latter best known by his surname of Bacchiacca), Giovanni di Pietro (called Lo Spagna), Andrea di Luigi (called L'Ingegno), Eusebio di San Giorgio, Benedetto Caporali, and others. We have already noted Bernardino di Betto, called Pinturicchio, as his assistant, and later as a sort of partner and superintendent of these young apprentices; and there seems little doubt that, after the completion of the Cambio frescoes and Perugino's subsequent return to Florence, Pinturicchio took young Rafaelle with him to Siena, as an assistant in his great commission there (1502) to decorate the library of Cardinal Piccolomini. In Perugino the brilliant but most assimilative young student found just the master he needed. He would have been crushed under the masterful force, the relentless nudities, of such a master as Luca

Signorelli, whereas in Pietro's devotional art, with its accurate training in drawing, colour, and perspective, his sunny nature found room to expand, and his first visit to Florence (1504) proved as inspiring to him as it had been to his master.

Meanwhile that busy master, his decorative commission of the Sala del Cambio completed, had gone back at once to purely religious art in a great painting for the high altar at Vallombrosa, which is now in the Florence Accademia. The subject is the Assumption of Mary Virgin, who appears in a mandorla surrounded by angels, while God the Father bends to bless from heaven, and four saints on earth beneath await in adoration. This was probably painted at the monastery, for Vasari says distinctly, "At Vallombrosa he painted a picture for the high altar"; and this is quite likely, as well as that his two grand profile portraits of the Abbot Baldasarre and of Don Biagio Milanesi date from the same visit.

We have already noticed his finely virile portrait of Francesco delle Opere in the Uffizi collection, and this, combined with the two monastic portraits just mentioned, now in the Florentine Accademia, proves that, if our master had devoted himself to portrait work, he might have been one of the greatest portraitists of all time. In the two last portraits the technique is of extreme simplicity. It is simply the bare shaven head, seen in profile against a brown background. But the drawing is faultless, the man himself is there, and there is not a touch more than is needed to reveal the bones of the skull beneath an upper surface covering of flesh and skin.

The Vallombrosan altar-piece dates from 1500, and in 1501 Perugino was one of the Priors (Priori), and, being obliged to reside in the Communal Palace and give the most of his time to magisterial and civic duties, he probably had little time left for painting. But he took occasion to contract for future work (1502) – for saints and angels to be painted around a fine crucifix in wood for the Convent of S. Francesco al Monte, which is now in the Perugian Gallery; for designs for the intarsia work of S. Agostino, and a double altar-piece for the same church, as well as a Sposalizio (Marriage of Mary) for the Duomo.

In 1503 we have seen that Pietro had returned to Florence, and taken lodgings in the Pinti quarter. There followed the quarrel with Michelangelo which I have mentioned, and very shortly after this he left Florence again for Perugia. While here, he received a letter from the Priors of his birthplace, Città della Pieve, inviting him to paint a fresco there. This was on February 20, 1504, and, after some correspondence as to terms, in March following the contract was concluded, and the fresco painted in the same year. The subject of this fine fresco is the Adoration of the Magi. Hidden away in its little township, it is not easily accessible to visitors, and escaped the plunder of the French. I have not yet been able to visit it, but my friend Dr. G. C. Williamson, who drove to Città across the mountains from Perugia, was deeply impressed by the painting and the place, and writes, "The town is strangely beautiful – like a petrified city, left high and dry by the moving waters of civilisation, untouched and unspoiled." At Panicale, another township near there, is a St. Sebastian by our master, signed and dated 1505. These were works which he probably painted rapidly and for a comparatively low price – the Pieve Adoration having been reduced to seventy-five florins – and Crowe and Cavalcaselle trace the hand of his assistant, Lo Spagna, in the Panicale St. Sebastian and an Assumption in that city.

But Perugino had by no means abandoned Florence as yet, for we find him writing from there in June of 1505 to the Marchioness of Mantua to acknowledge the receipt of eighty ducats for his tempera painting of the "Combat of Love and Chastity."

Isabella d'Este da Gonzaga, Marchioness of Mantua, an enthusiastic collector and art patron, and one of the most cultivated women of her time, was at that moment forming within her palace at Mantua the famous Studio della Grotta, which she adorned with paintings by Mantegna, Costa, and Perugino. These paintings, which I have described in my own work on Mantua, and elsewhere, were still in the Grotta in 1627, but after the terrible sack of Mantua in 1630 they were sold to Cardinal Richelieu, and are now in the Musée du Louvre. They were all of allegorical subjects, dictated by the Marchesa herself, and the "Parnassus" of her court painter, Andrea Mantegna, is a masterpiece. But that of the Perugian master is far less satisfactory, and was indeed found so by that very keen critic, the Marchesa Isabella herself. She wrote to him on June 30 of the year 1505: "The picture has reached me safely, and, as it is well drawn and coloured, pleases me; but if it had been more carefully finished, it would have been more to your honour and our satisfaction." She here goes straight to the point in noting – as we shall do later – that the master was becoming careless and hasty in his execution. On the other hand, it is fair to remember that the subject was not probably congenial, that he was tied hand and foot in his treatment by the learned lady's written instructions (on hearing that he had represented Venus as nude, she declared that if one single figure were altered the whole fable would be ruined), and it is only in the wide sweep of clear sky and hills and river that the artist really finds himself again.

Another commission of this time in Florence was to complete the Descent from the Cross begun in 1503 by Filippino Lippi, and left unfinished at his death in 1505. This picture, which was destined for the SS. Annunziata at Florence, was completed by Perugino, and is now in the Accademia. The lower portion is here by our master, and, considering the initial difficulty of working upon another man's conception, the result is to be praised. Crowe, indeed, calls the Virgin fainting in the arms of the three Maries one of the noblest conceptions of his brush. But the same cannot be said of his joint commission of the Assumption, painted also for the SS. Annunziata in this summer of 1505. Dr. Williamson, whose monograph I have already mentioned, and who went to the pains of visiting all these works of Perugino scattered by Napoleon through the small provincial museums of France, noted that the resemblance between the Assumption and the Ascension of Lyons, which had been painted in 1495 for S. Pietro at Perugia, is so close as to show the artist had hardly troubled to make any change. Not only this, but the Coronation of the Virgin, of the Perugian Gallery, shows groups identical with both the above paintings, and this Assumption, for which, as Crowe says, "he fell back on the model of the Lyons Ascension," is painted in a slovenly and careless manner.

When we remember what Florence was in this early sixteenth century – a city keenly intellectual, alive to art as perhaps no city, save Athens, has ever been before or since, and highly critical and censorious – we need not be surprised that the master, thus openly convicted of plagiarism from his earlier works and of careless technique, was censured by his friends and attacked by his enemies. Vasari tells us that "when the aforesaid work" (the Assumption) "was uncovered, it was freely blamed by all the younger craftsmen, and, in particular, because Pietro had made use of those figures which had already appeared in his other works; and his friends replied that it was not that his powers had failed, but that he had acted so either from greed of money or from haste. To whom Pietro answered: 'I have put into this work the figures praised before by you, and with which you were infinitely pleased. If now they displease you and are not praised, what can I do to help it?' But these men continued to assail him with sonnets and public insults. Whence he, already old, left Florence, and returned to Perugia." There is something pathetic in the old man's reply, and it must have cost him a heart-pang to thus turn his back on Florence. He had loved the city, had gained there his first inspiration in art, his first successes, had wedded there, bought a house and property, and purchased in this noble Church of the SS. Annunziata a burial-place for himself and his descendants. But he never returned. His name disappears from the rolls of the painters' guild in Florence, and in 1506 appears in that of Perugia. Umbria welcomed back her great master with reverent appreciation. That divided impulse of his life was ended, and from henceforth he was all her own.

Always a good man of business, Perugino's first step on reaching Perugia was to collect the debts still due to him. From the authorities of Città della Pieve he demanded the balance (March of 1507) of 25 florins, which was liquidated by the conveyance of a house, from Panicale 11 florins, and for his work in the Cambio he drew 350 ducats. Then the commissions began to come in again, and an altar-piece of this very time (1507), representing Madonna between SS. Jerome and Francis, has recently come to the London National Gallery from the Palazzo Penna at Perugia, and is a work of charm and great merit. It had been ordered in 1507 by the executors of Giovanni Schiavone, a master-carpenter of Perugia, to be set over the altar of a chapel in S. Maria de' Servi in that city. This work completed, he left for Foligno, where I found still in place his fresco of The Baptism of Christ in the Church of La Nunziatella, and from Foligno (1507-8) he was summoned by Pope Julius to Rome to decorate the ceilings of his Vatican Palace. Bazzi (Sodoma) and Peruzzi were already being employed on the same work, and at Rome Perugino met his old friends and rivals in art – Signorelli, Bramantino, and others – and introduced to them his own pupil Caporali. When Rafaelle was accepted by Julius II. as his final and only master in the Vatican, and bidden by the impetuous Pontiff to destroy all work of other artists, he spared – with that *gentilezza* which was in his character – the ceiling paintings of his old master Perugino, which yet remain to us in the Camera dell' Incendio. But, eclipsed by his brilliant young pupil, there was clearly no room for old Pietro at Rome, and he journeyed northward with Signorelli, breaking his journey to paint a Crucifixion for S. Maria degli Angeli at Assisi, and another painting at Siena of the same subject for the Church of S. Agostino. A fragment which is in the collection of Miss Hertz at Rome may belong to another picture due to this Siena visit; and later we find him painting at Bettona, and (1512-13) in his own birthplace of Città della Pieve.

Vasari has a gossiping story that Pietro, "who trusted no one, and, in going and returning from Castello della Pieve, carried all the money he had about him always on his person," was robbed on the way, and lost his money and nearly his life. And he adds next: "Pietro was a person of very little religion, and could never be made to believe in the immortality of the soul; nay, with words adapted to his evil mind, he did most obstinately refuse every good path. He placed all his hopes in the goods of fortune, and for money would have made every bad contract." There were two reasons why Vasari should have been unfair to Perugino – one, that he was an Umbrian, even though long resident in Florence, the other, that he had come, as we have seen, into collision with his admired Michelangelo. Even so, Vasari is much too good a judge to depreciate his art, but he attacks the Perugian master personally, and his remarks about religion do not count for much. Vasari lived in an age – that of the counter-Reformation – which combined in Italy the lowest level of morals with apparent orthodoxy, and, under the shadow of the Inquisition, religion became a good stone to throw at your enemy. But we cannot say there is nothing behind his charge, because, with regret, we have seen within these pages this master of the tender virgins and calm saints of God as being vindictive (that affair before the Eight with Aulista di Angelo comes to our thought), disloyal, and shifty in his business dealings (here the Orvietans and their Chapel of S. Brizio are an instance), and always consistently keen on getting the best side of a bargain. It does come as something of a shock – at any rate to me – to turn from this serenely devotional art to this record of the man's personality, and we feel inclined to echo the words of Symonds, who asks, "How could such a man have endured to pass a long life in the fabrication of devotional pictures?" The answer perhaps lies in the fact that Pietro did not create this lovely art of devotion, of which he was such a supreme interpreter. He found it all around him, in the aspirations of thousands of prayerful souls, even in the very soil of this land of his, where the Etruscans had once quarried the tombs of their dead, and as an art motive it absorbed his whole feeling. When, later in life, material success came to invade his nature, its influence as a corrosive at once appears in his art creation. The touch of ideal beauty leaves his figures; drawing, colour, composition become mere hasty repetition of his earlier efforts.

And yet we cannot but think of the old master with pleasure, even in these later years, as filling these little hill-towns of Umbria, Bettona, Assisi, Montefalco, Spello, Trevi, most of all his own birthplace, Castello della Pieve, with frescoes which are at least lovely shadows of his greatest works. At Bettona he had painted a St. Anthony, and again in the Church of S. Peter at Città della Pieve, and here, too, in the Church of S. Maria de' Servi is the fragment – but a beautiful fragment – of a ruined Crucifixion. The frescoes of S. Maria Maggiore at Spello (signed and dated 1521), and the Adoration of the Magi in the Church of S. Maria delle Lagrime at Trevi, are important in this late period of his art, as well as perhaps a Nativity in the Church of S. Francesco at Montefalco, which is filled with work of his pupils. But a work of special interest is his completion of the frescoes of his greatest pupil, Rafaelle of Urbino, in the Church of S. Severo at Perugia. Sixteen years had elapsed since Rafaelle in 1505 had, as a youth of brilliant promise, painted the upper fresco, anticipating therein the composition of his great Disputa del Sacramento within the Vatican. Since then he had gone on from strength to strength, and now, in his declining years, his old master was called on to complete his pupil's work. The six saints whom he painted there, beneath Rafaelle's fresco, grouped on either side of terra-cotta figures of the Virgin and Child – SS. Jerome, John, Gregory, and Boniface, with SS. Scolastica and Martha – possess, as far as can be now judged, both dignity and beauty. The fresco is signed by him, and dated with the year of 1521, little more than a year before his death.

For to the last the old man was busy, and after a long life of industry died almost with the brush within his hand. This very year of 1521 he was at Trevi as well as Spello. In 1522 he painted the "Transfiguration" for S. Maria Nuova at Perugia, and his frescoes for the Convent of S. Agnese at Perugia, which are still in place – both the "Transfiguration" and its three predella panels being now in the Perugian Gallery. His last work (1523), the fresco of the Adoration of the Shepherds (a fresco now transferred to canvas), is now in the London National Gallery, where is also his charming Virgin with the little Jesus and St. John, a signed work from the late Mr. Beckford's collection. The child Jesus stands, naked and upright, upon a stone balustrade, and plays with a lock of His mother's hair, who is herself of the pure virginal type imaged by Rafaelle in his earlier creations, notably the famous "Madonna del Granduca"; while the "Adoration," the master's last work, was removed from the Church of Fontignano in 1843. The landscape in both these works – in the Beckford Virgin blue hills and outlined trees, in the Fontignano fresco wide-sweeping uplands – is of great attraction.

> "As the aged artist," says Crowe, "laboured at Fontignano, industrious to the close, a plague broke out in the Perugia district and ravaged the country. A disgraceful panic over-spread the land. It was decreed that the ceremonies of religion should be omitted in all cases where death ensued from the contagion. Perugino died and was buried in a field at Fontignano … and no one knows where lie the bones of Pietro Perugino."

Later documentary evidence, which is quoted by the above authors, and at greater length by Milanesi in his edition of "Vasari's Lives," has here overthrown the statement by Vasari that "Pietro, having come to the age of seventy-two years, ended the course of his life in Castello della Pieve, where he was honourably buried in the year 1524." We know now that his sons (1524) endeavoured to have their father's body brought from his hasty burial-place to be interred in S. Agostino at Perugia; but, in the disturbed state of central Italy during this epoch of foreign invasion, the pious wish was never fulfilled.

When we think with what care and expense Pietro had once prepared his last resting-place in S. Maria de' Servi at Florence, this tragedy of his unknown and hurried burial seems the more sad. He survives in his art; and that is a complete vindication, an undying memorial. In these pages we have traced his progress from his first great commission of the Sistine Chapel, with its dignified grouping and sense of air and space, through the tender beauty of his altar-pieces, the simplicity and breadth of his fresco work – the Nativity of the Villa Albani, the Crucifixion of S. Maria Maddalena de' Pazzi, the Pietà of the nuns of S. Chiara, the altar-piece of the Certosa of Pavia – till, in his great decorative commission at Perugia of the Sala del Cambio, in the year 1500, he seemed to reach the summit of his creative power, and climb down from thence, though by no means immediately or conclusively, to these faded and yet exquisite frescoes, with which, in his own fading years, he wreathed the little hill-cities of his native Umbria. And we noted him as a complete master of his art, even though he might willingly abide within a certain religious convention; we saw that the master of the Delivery of the Keys within the Sistine, the great portrait artist, whose hand has left us those forceful heads of Francesco delle Opere, of the Abbot Baldasarre, and Don Biagio, the painter of the Albani and Certosa altar-pieces, the decorator of the Cambio, had nothing to fear in his powers of art creation from the very greatest of his time.

But after we have said all this, we must own that his special place within that galaxy of genius of the greatest Italian art is best described by a writer to whose appreciative criticism I have always given my sincere admiration; for Pietro's task it was "to create for the soul amid the pomps and passions of this world a resting-place of contemplation, tenanted by saintly and seraphic beings. No pain comes near the folk of his celestial city; no longing poisons their repose; they are not weary, and the wicked trouble them no more. Their cheerfulness is no less perfect than their serenity; like the shades of Hellas, they have drunk Lethæan waters from the river of content, and all remembrance of things sad or harsh has vanished from their minds…. In the best work of Perugino, the Renaissance set the seal of absolute perfection upon pietistic art."

On the following pages are some contemporaries of Perugino.

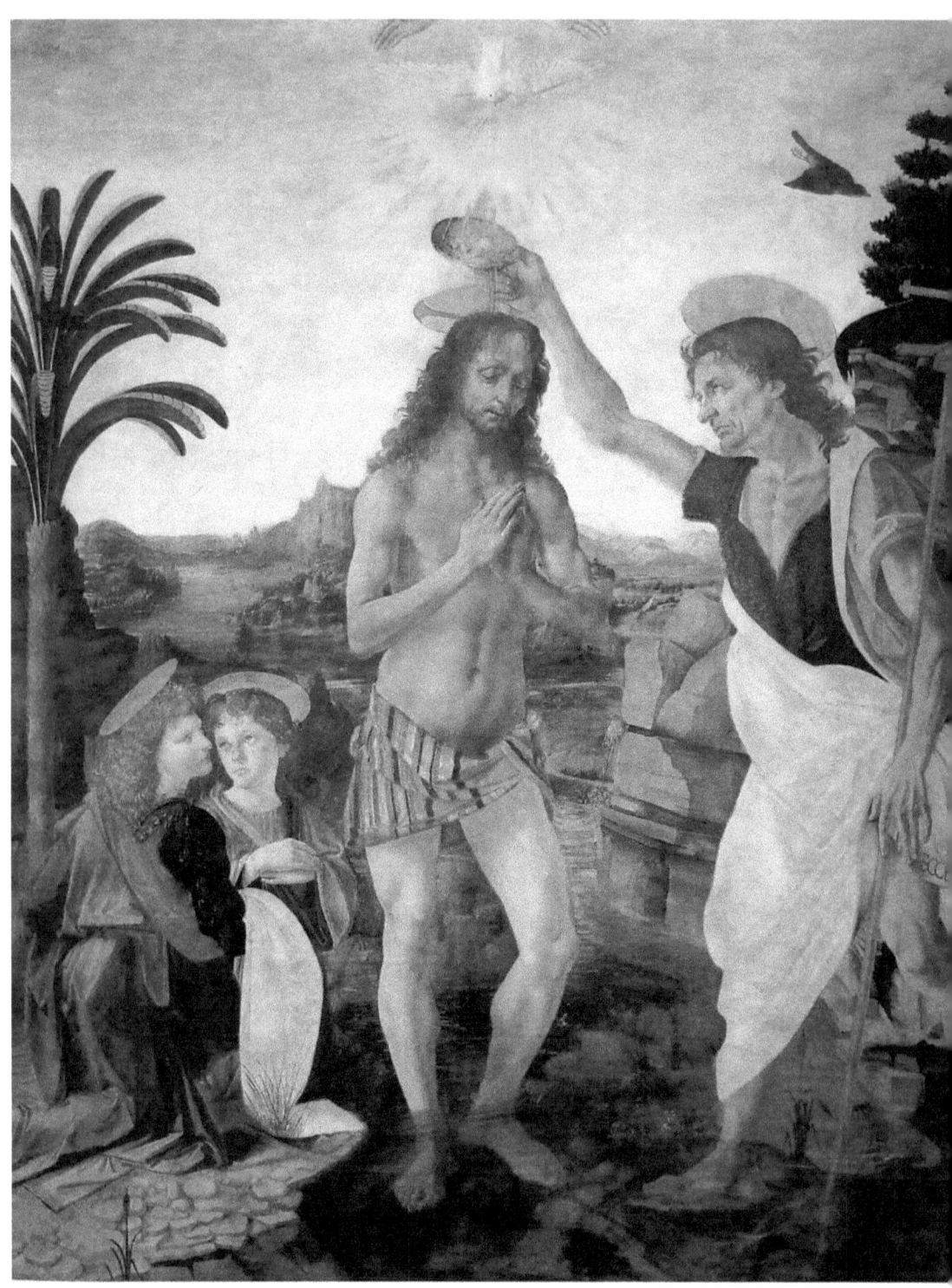

Andrea del Verrocchio, The Baptism of Christ

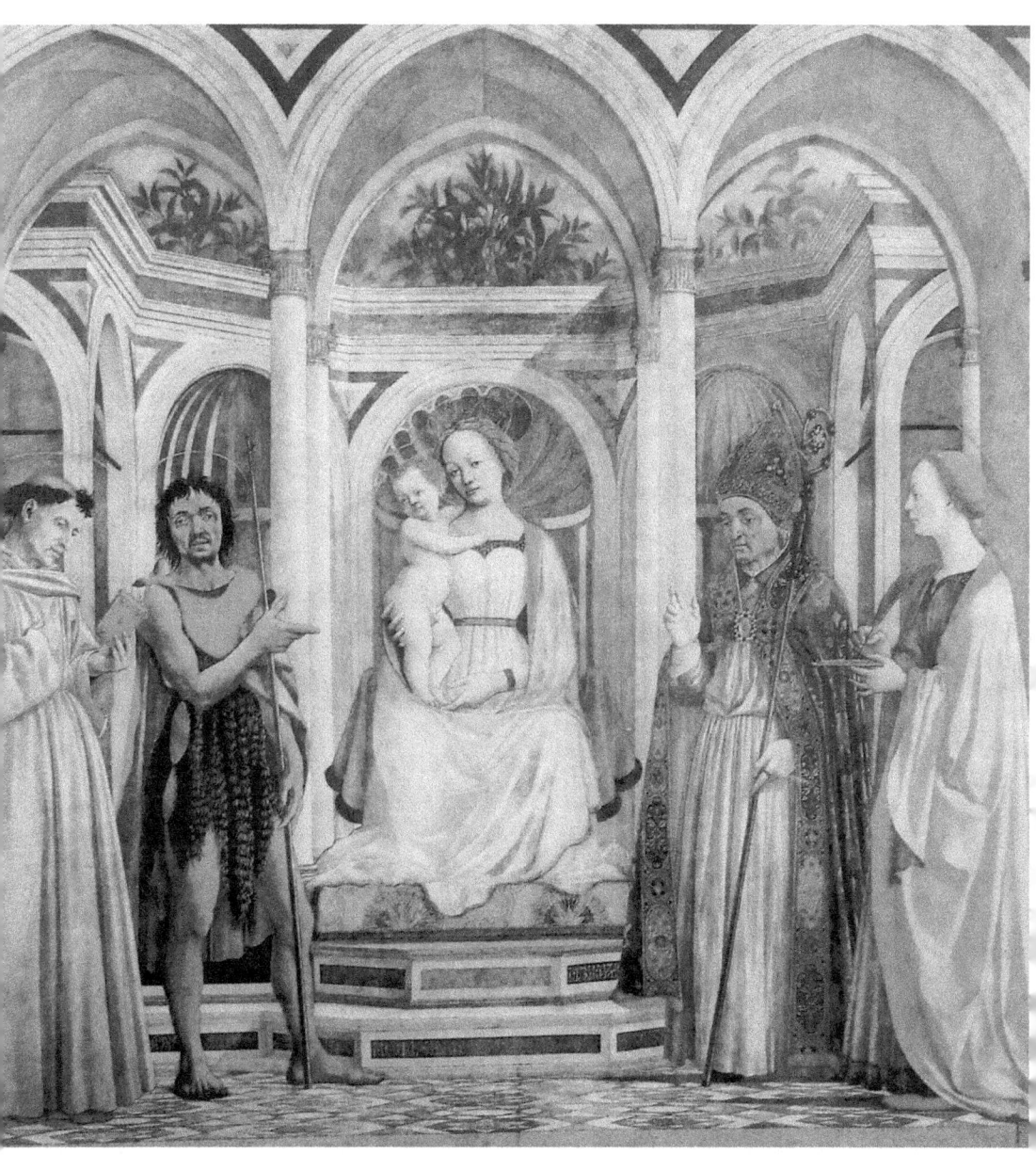

Domenico Veneziano, Madonna and Child With Saints, 1445, Uffizi Gallery

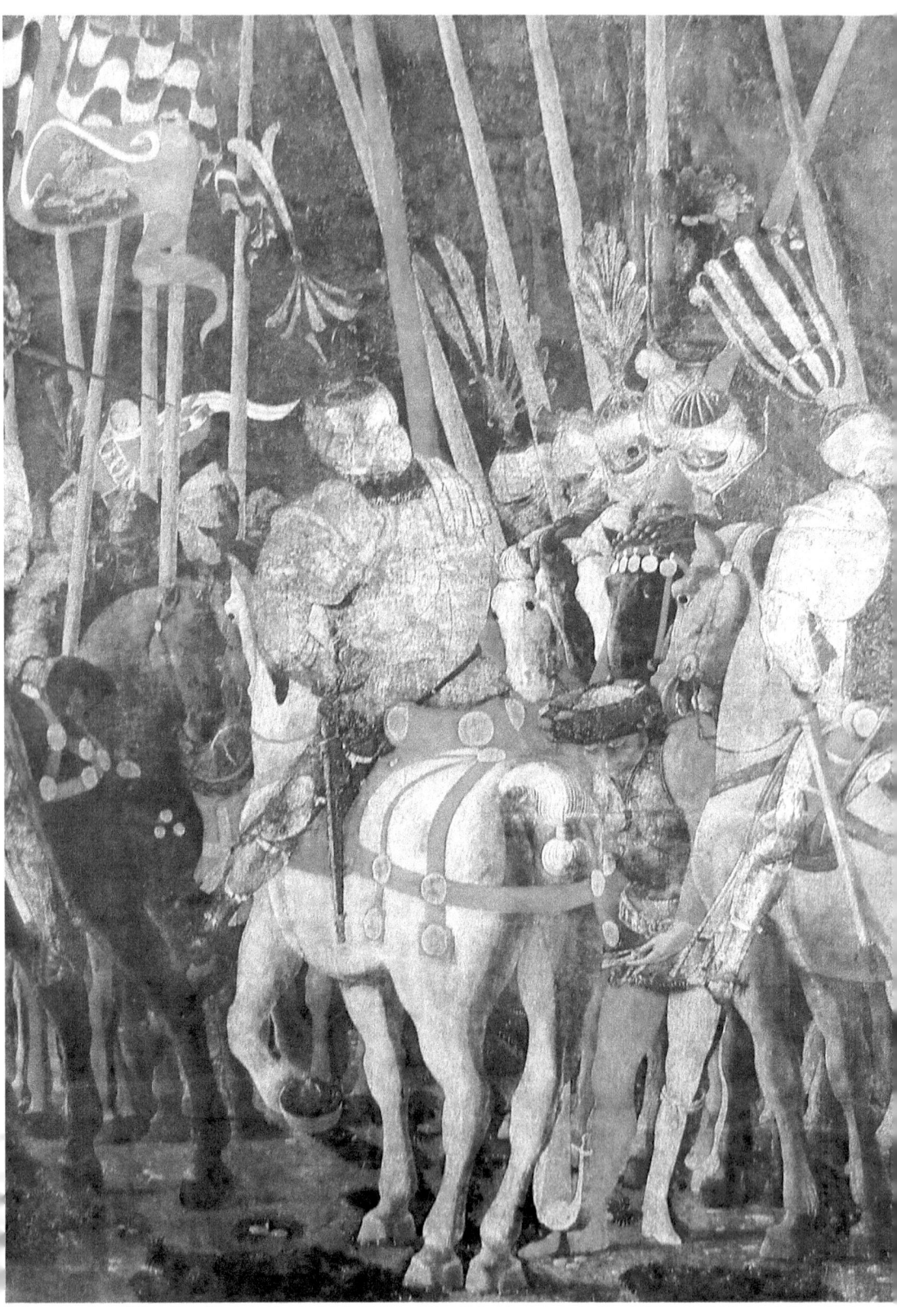

Paolo Uccello, The Battle of San Romano, Paris

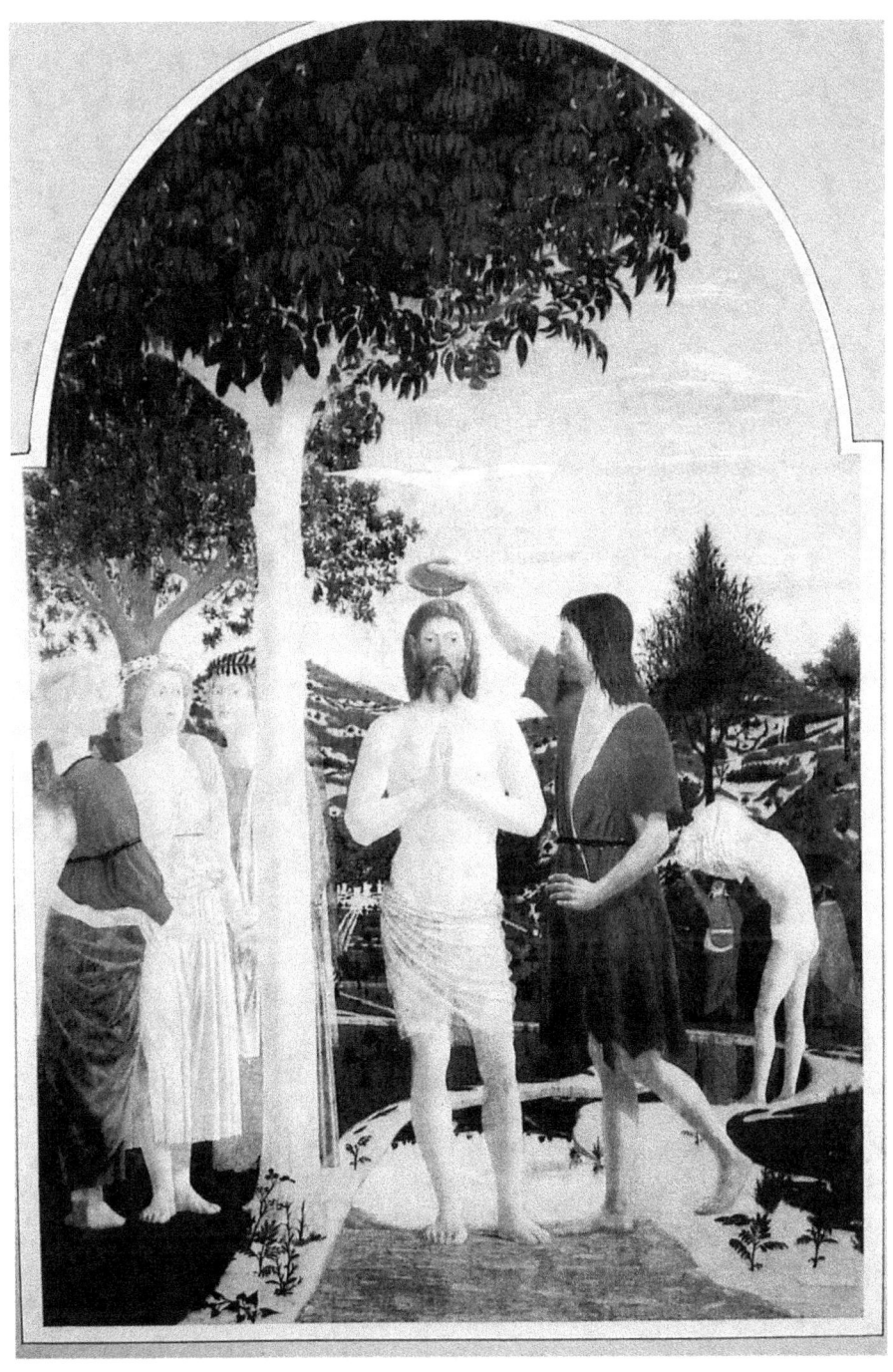

Piero della Francesca, *The Baptism of Christ*, National Gallery, London

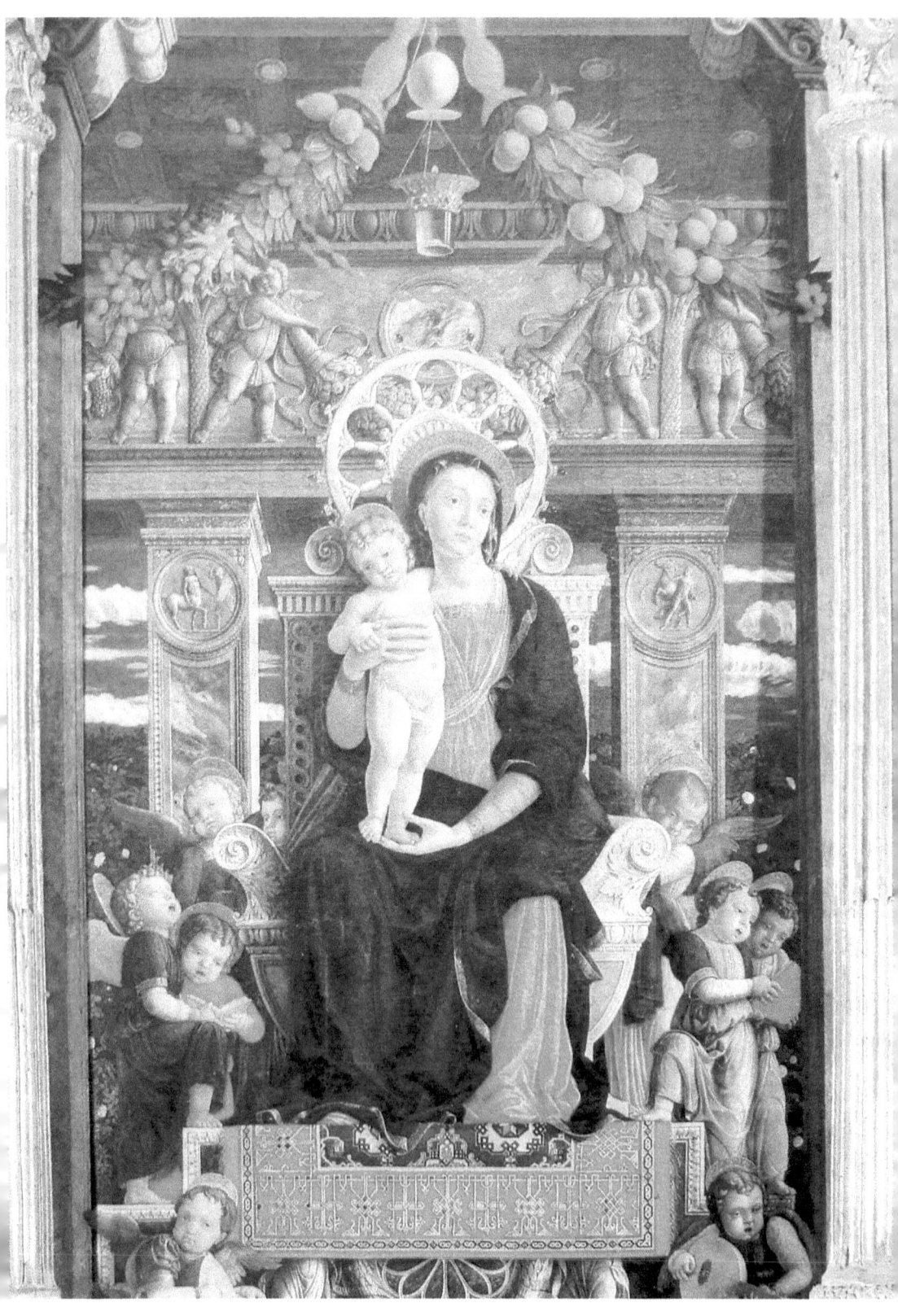

Andreas Mantegna, Madonna and Child Enthroned, 1457-60, Verona

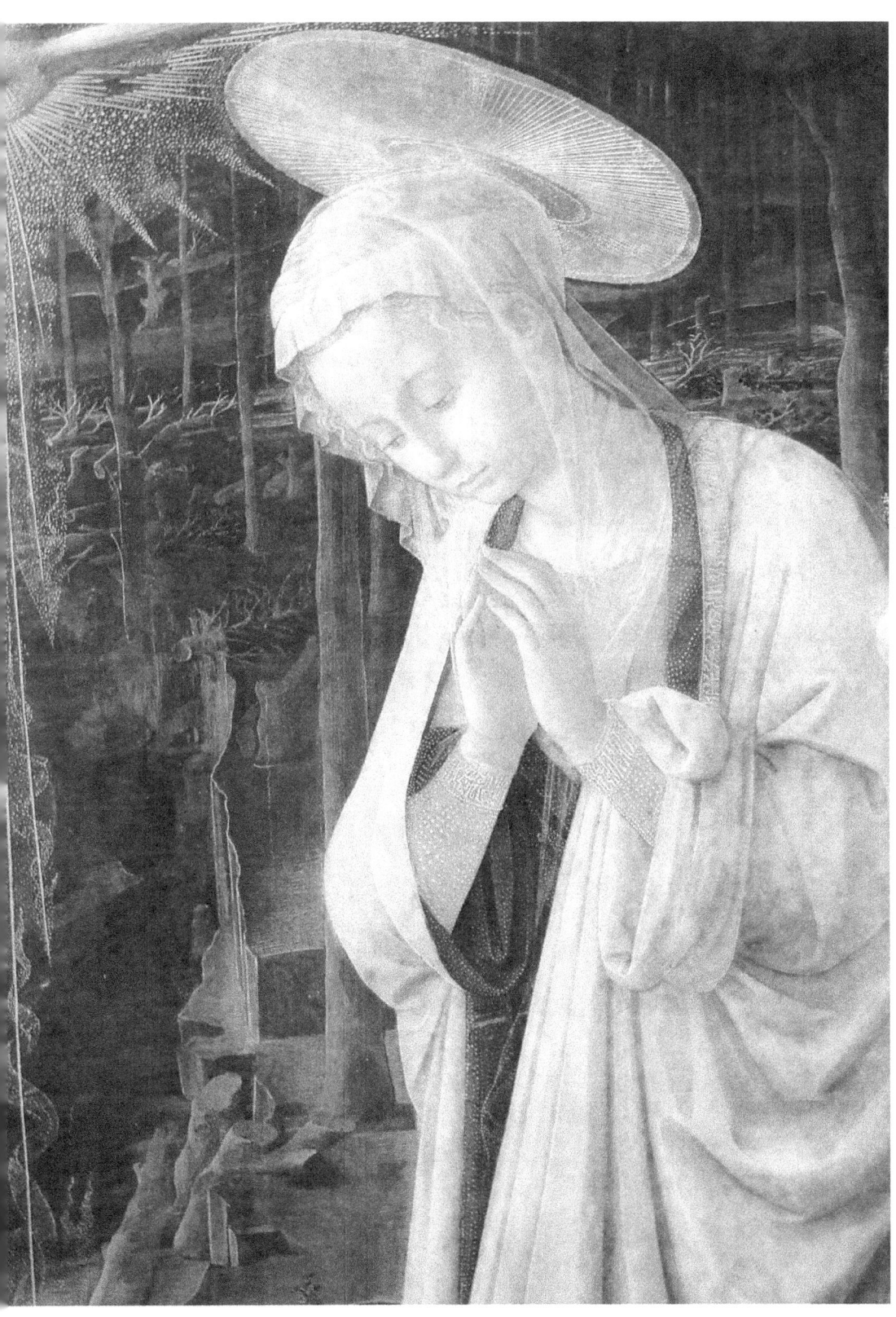

Fra Filippo Lippi, The Adoration of the Virgin, Berlin, detail

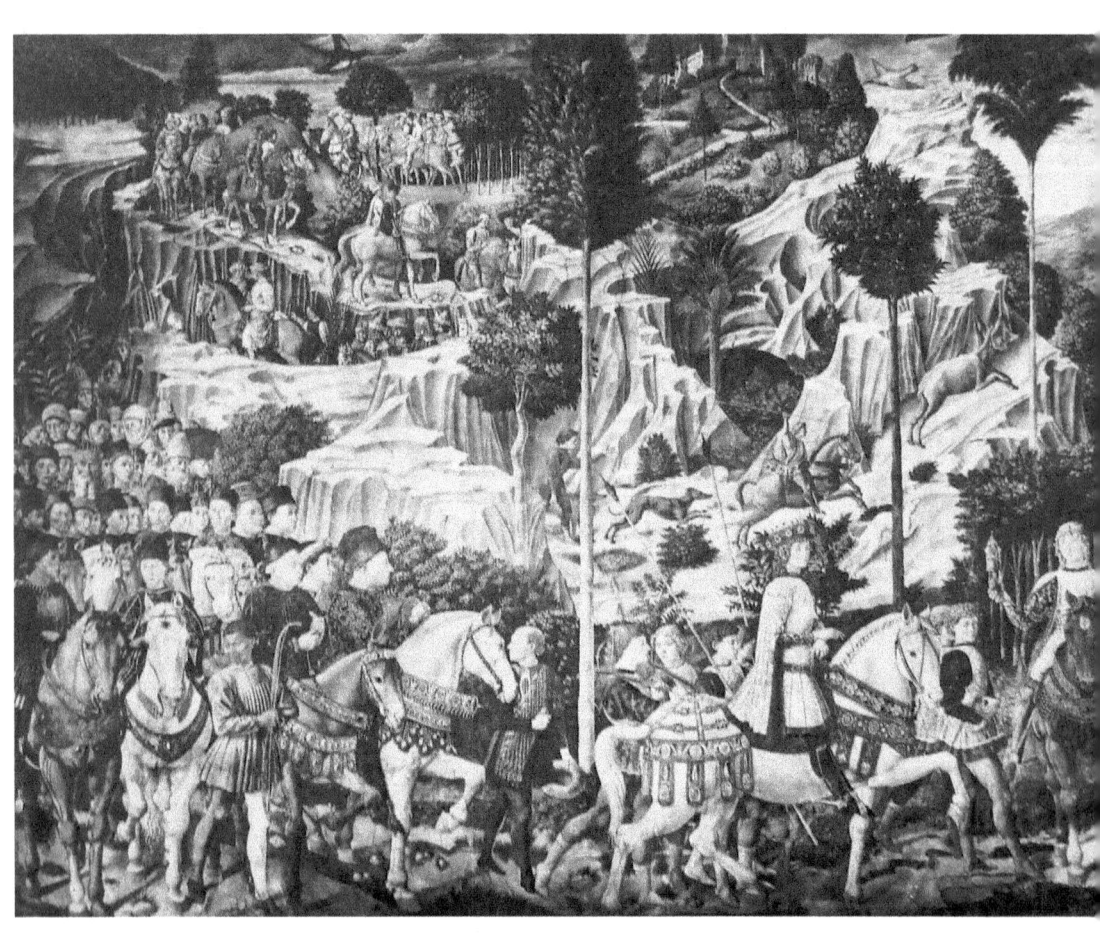

Benozzo Gozzoli, Journey of the Magi

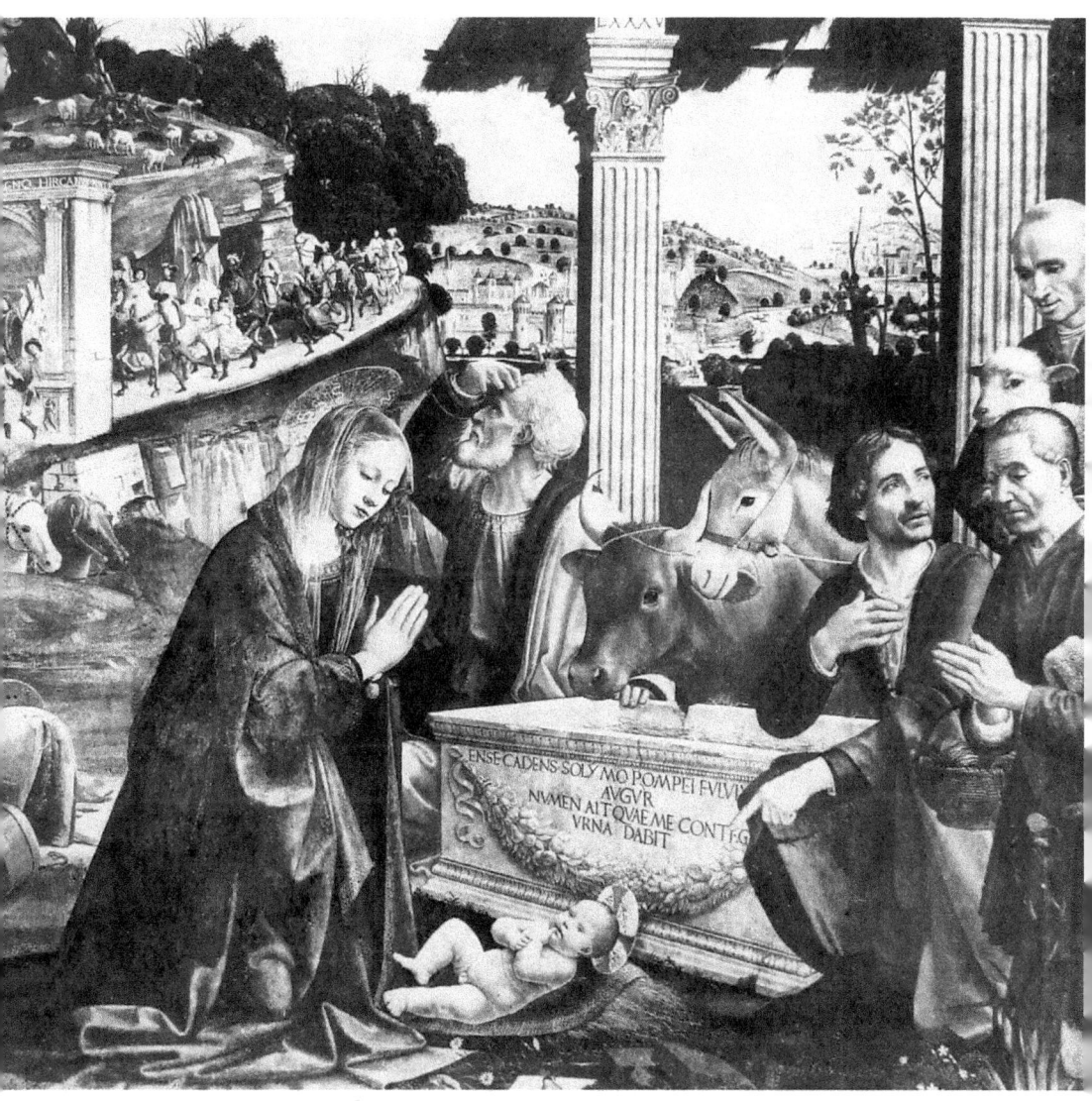

Domenico Ghirlandaio, Adoration of the Shepherds, 1485

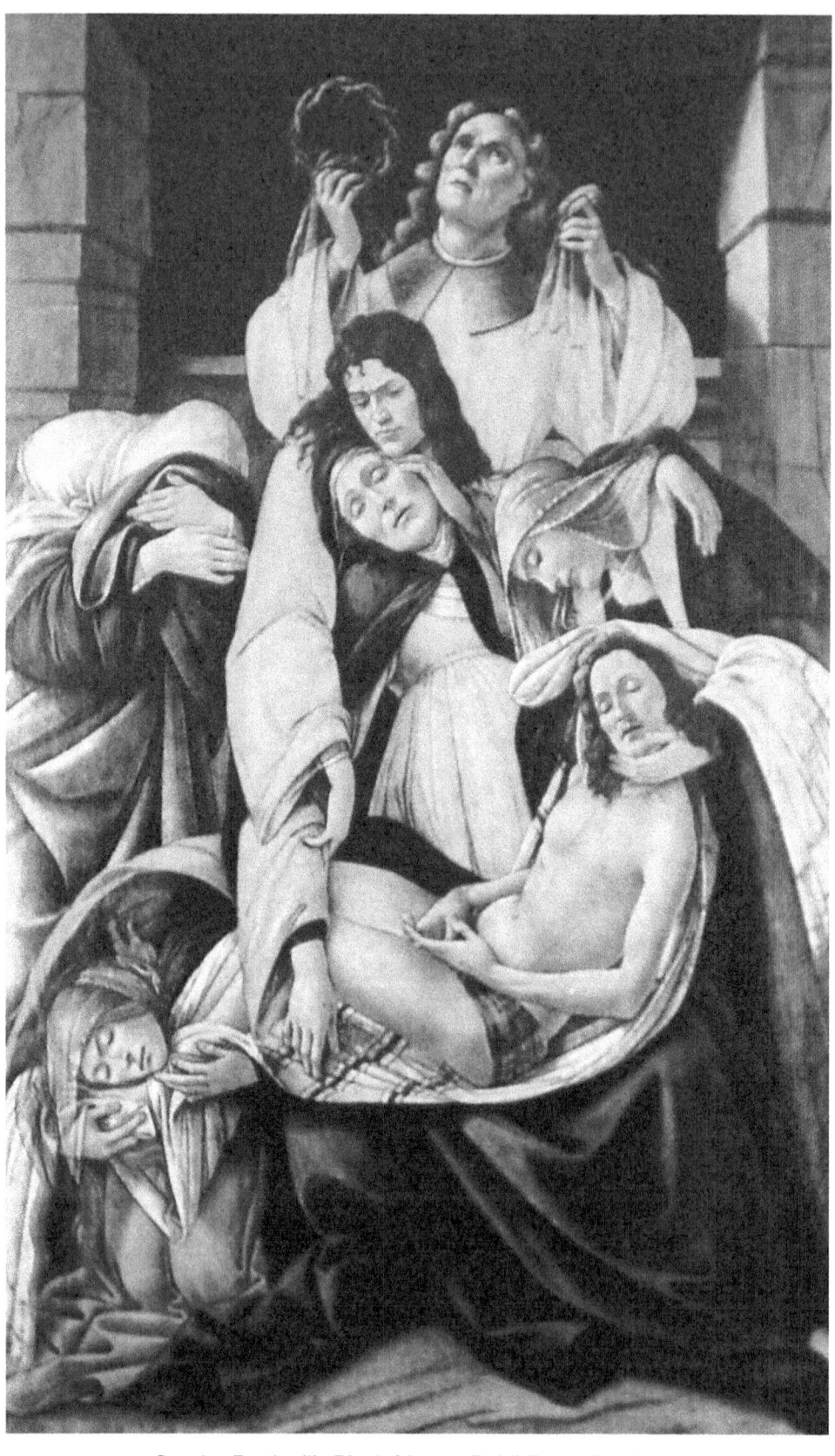

Sandro Botticelli, *Pietà*, Museo Poldi Pezzoli, Milan

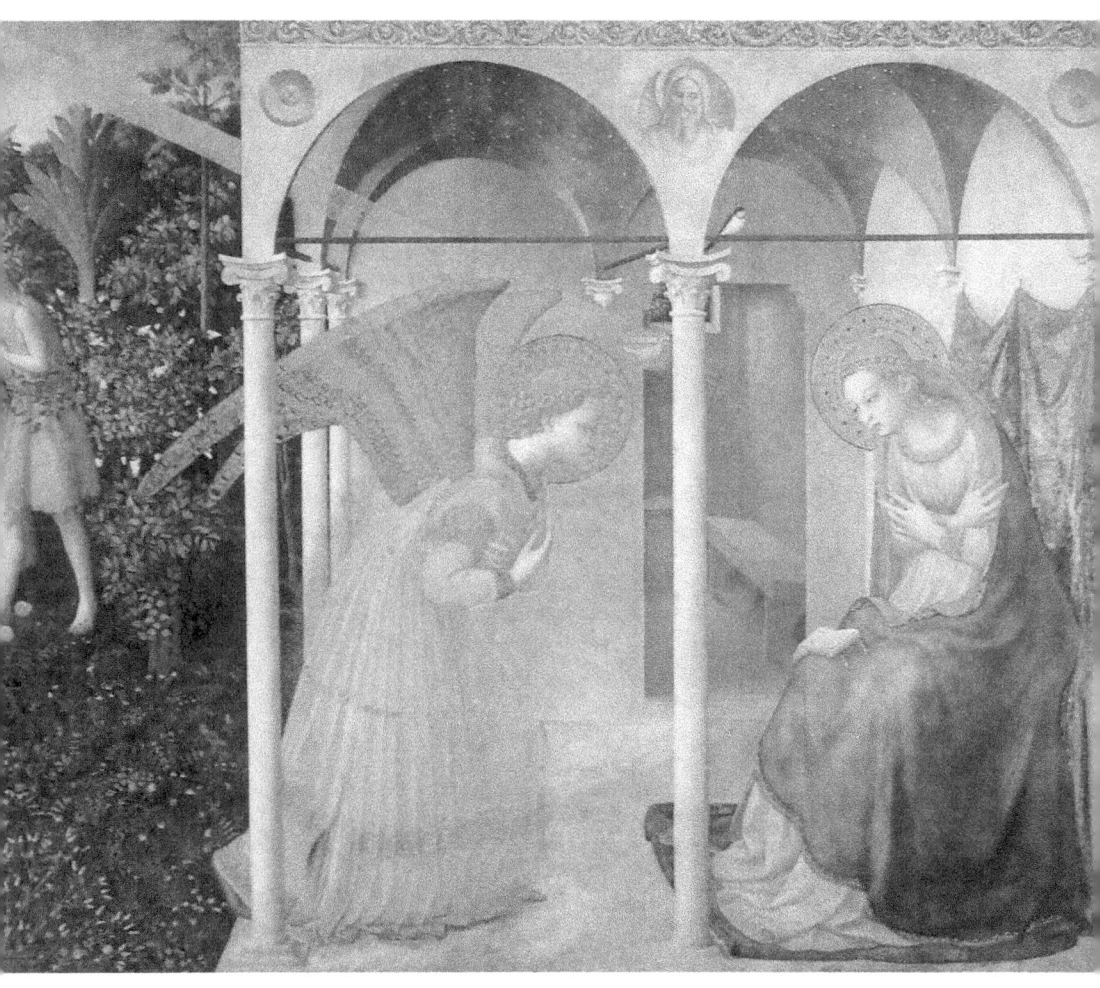

Fra Angelico, Annunciation, Prado, Madrid

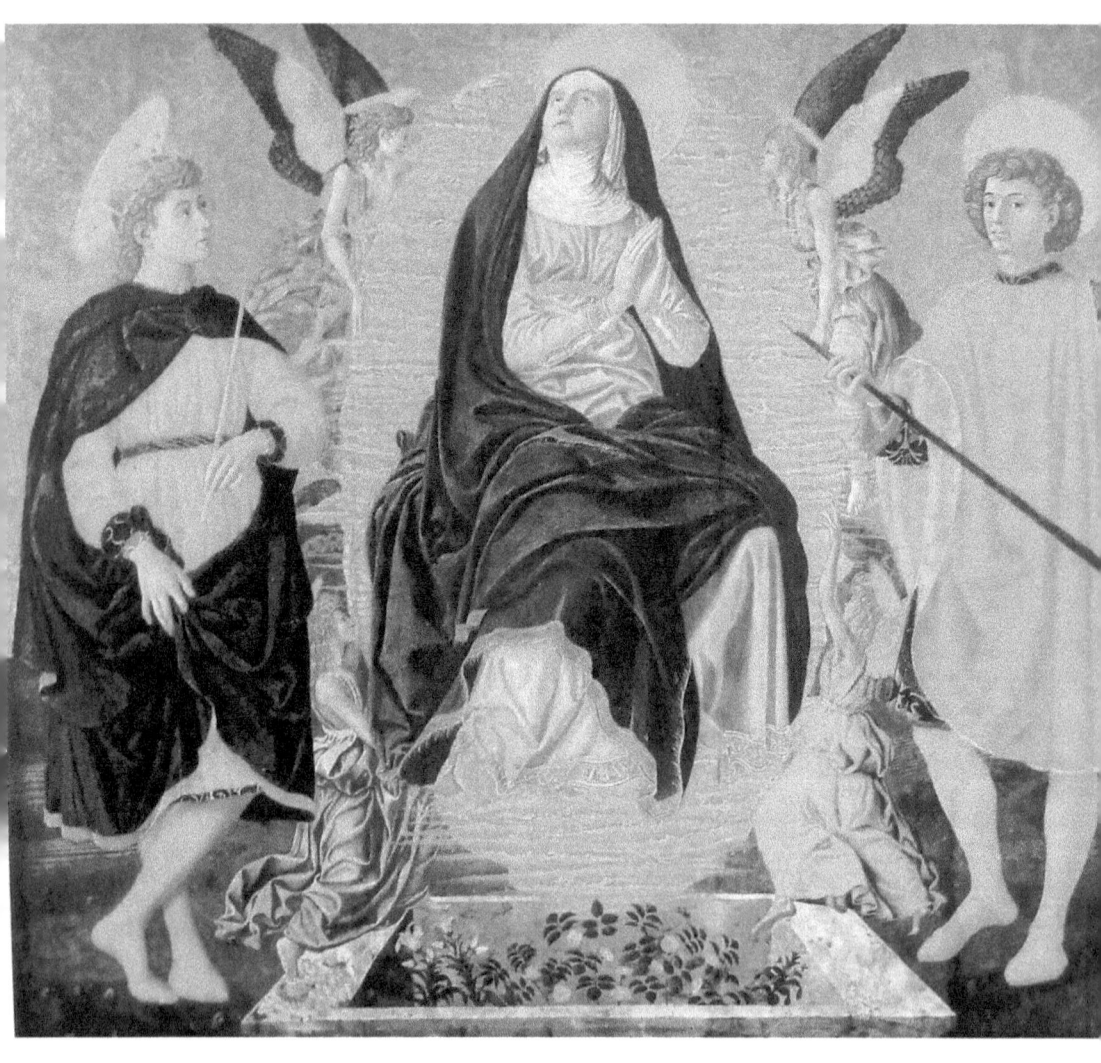

Andrea del Castagno, Assumption, Berlin

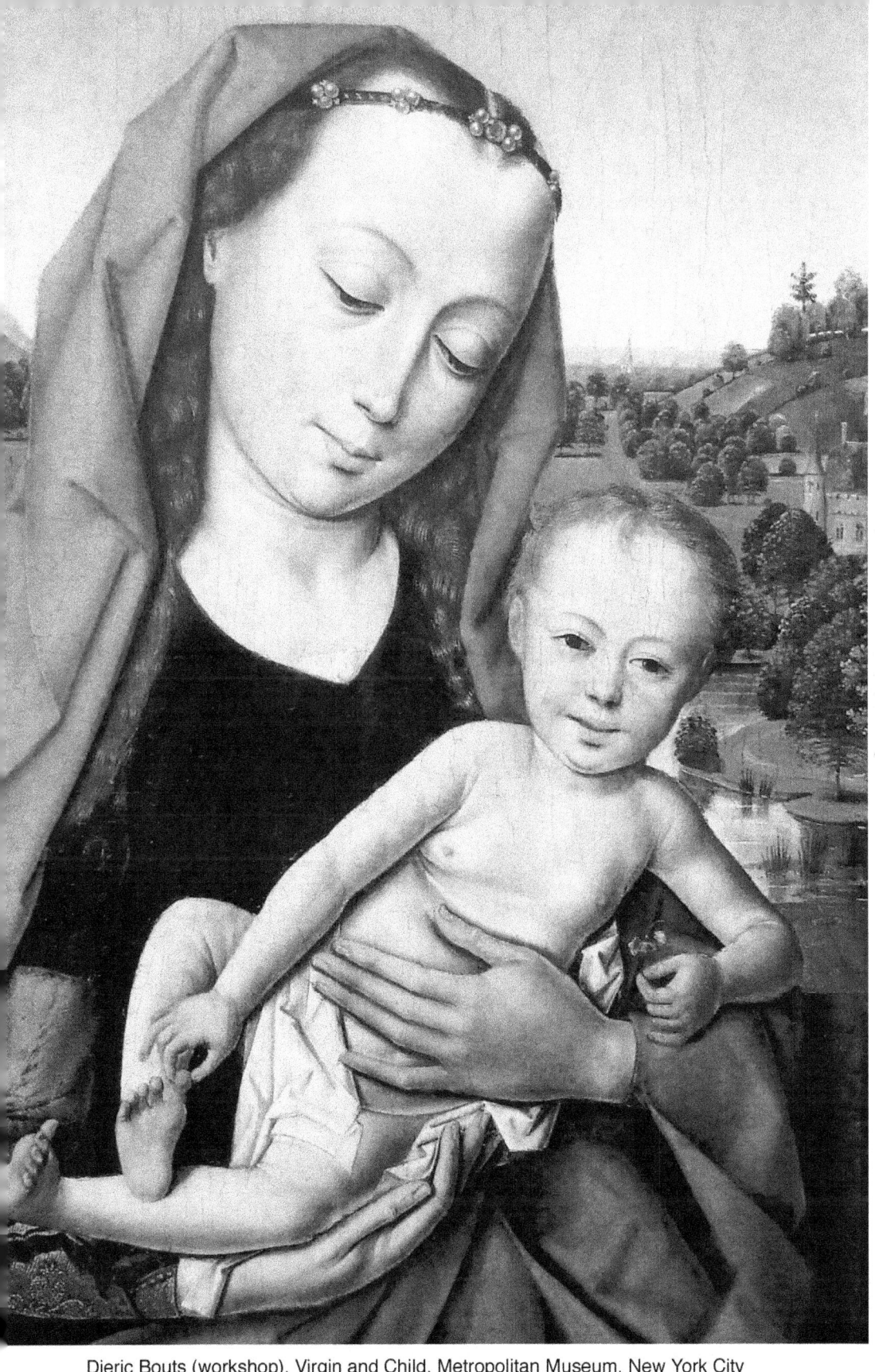

Dieric Bouts (workshop), Virgin and Child, Metropolitan Museum, New York City

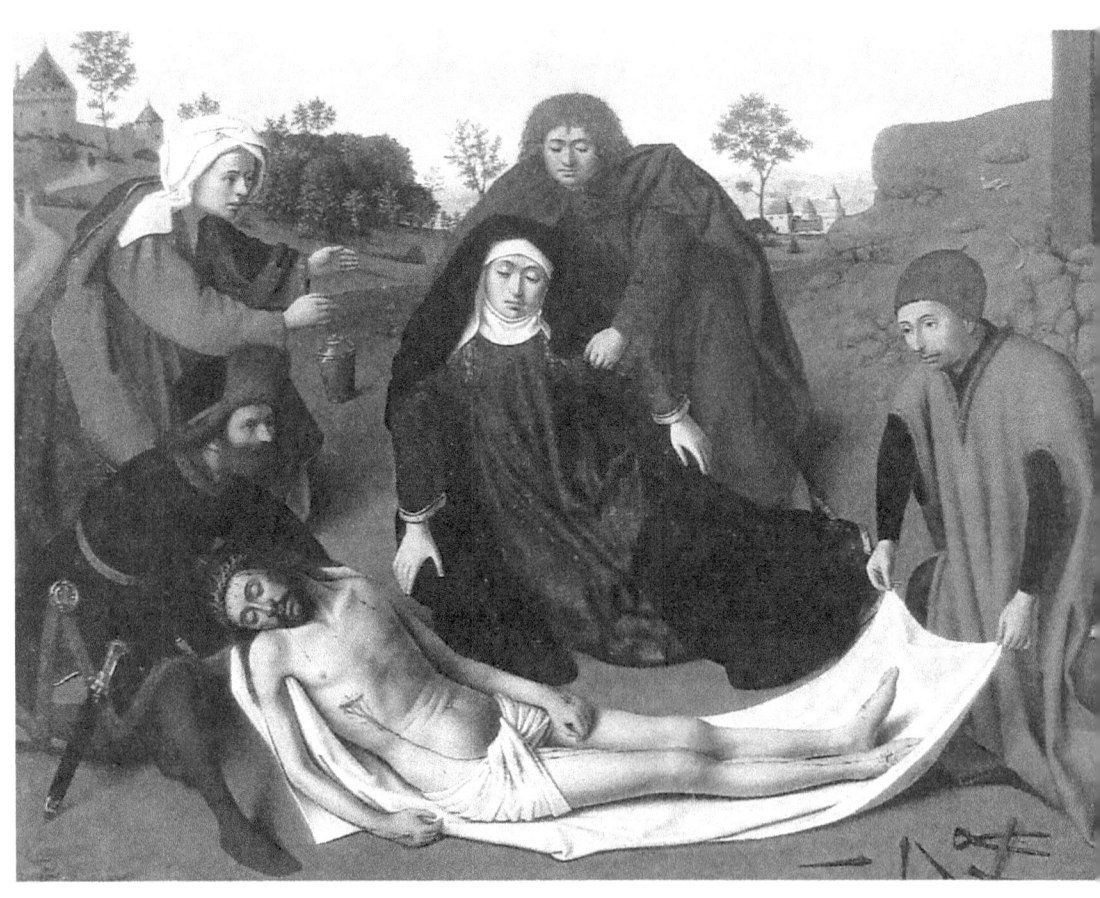

Petrus Christus, The Lamentation, Metropolitan Museum,
New York City

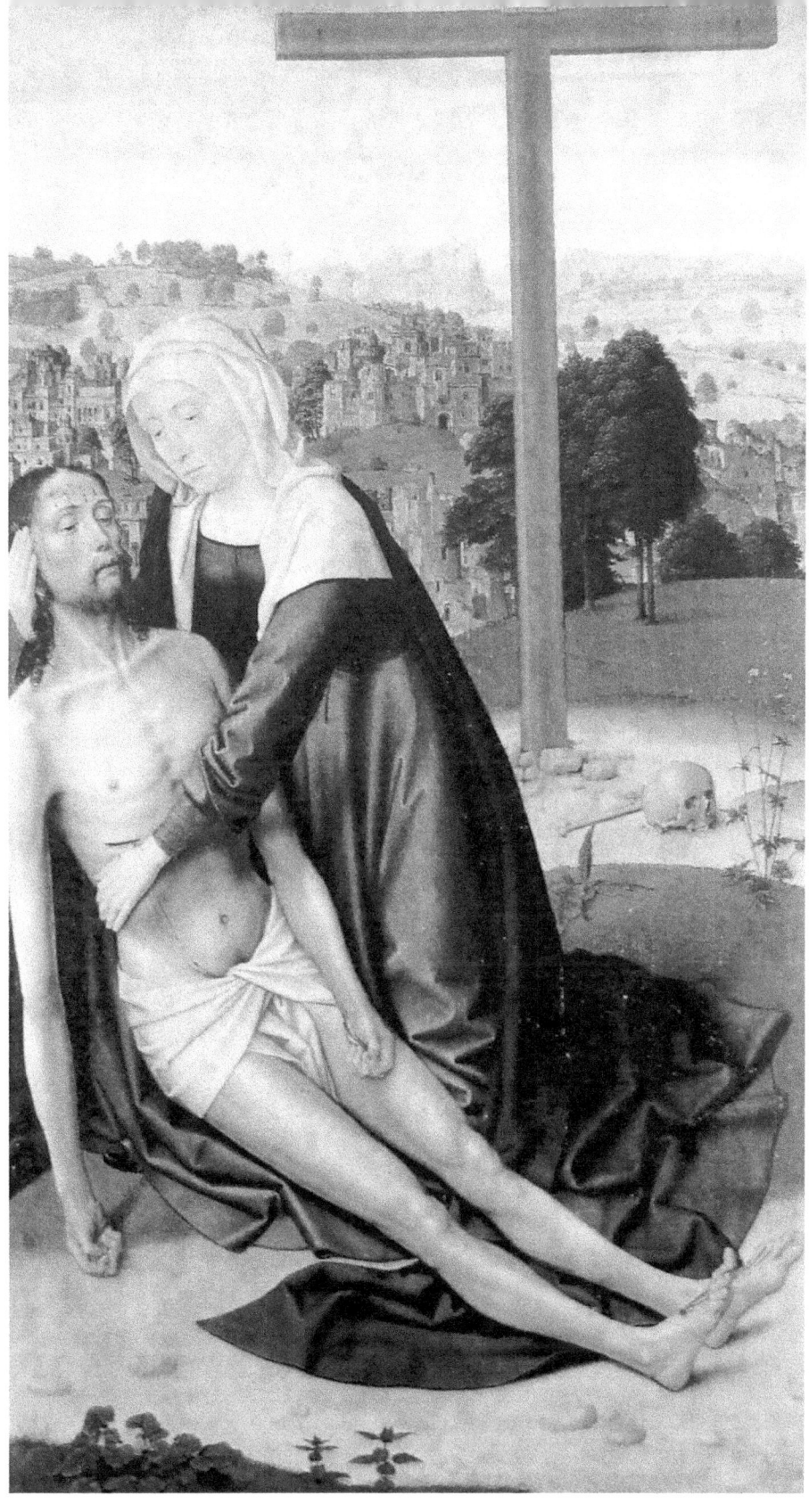

Gerard David, Pietà, Winterhur

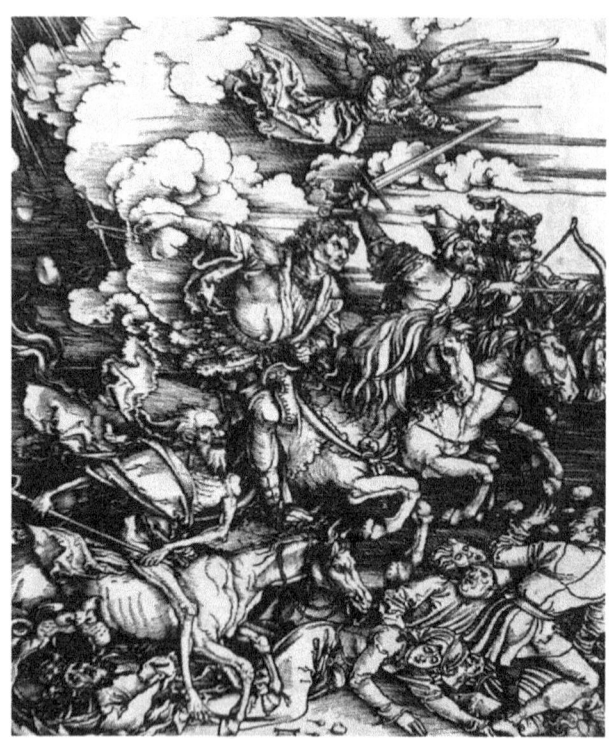

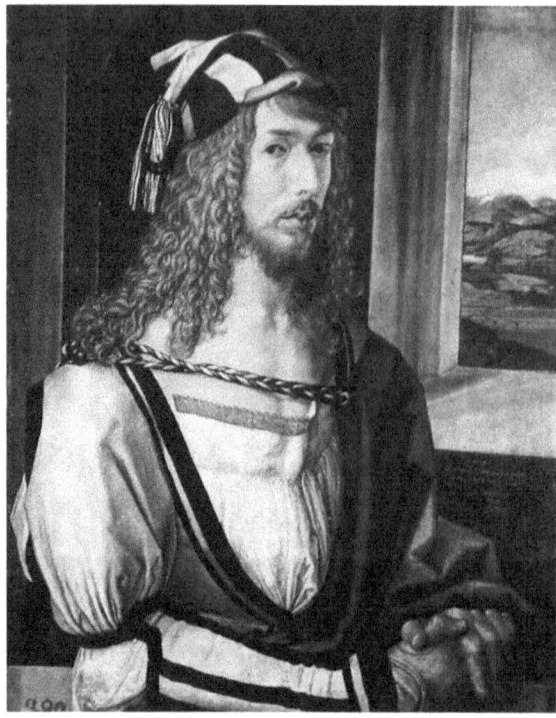

Albrecht Dürer

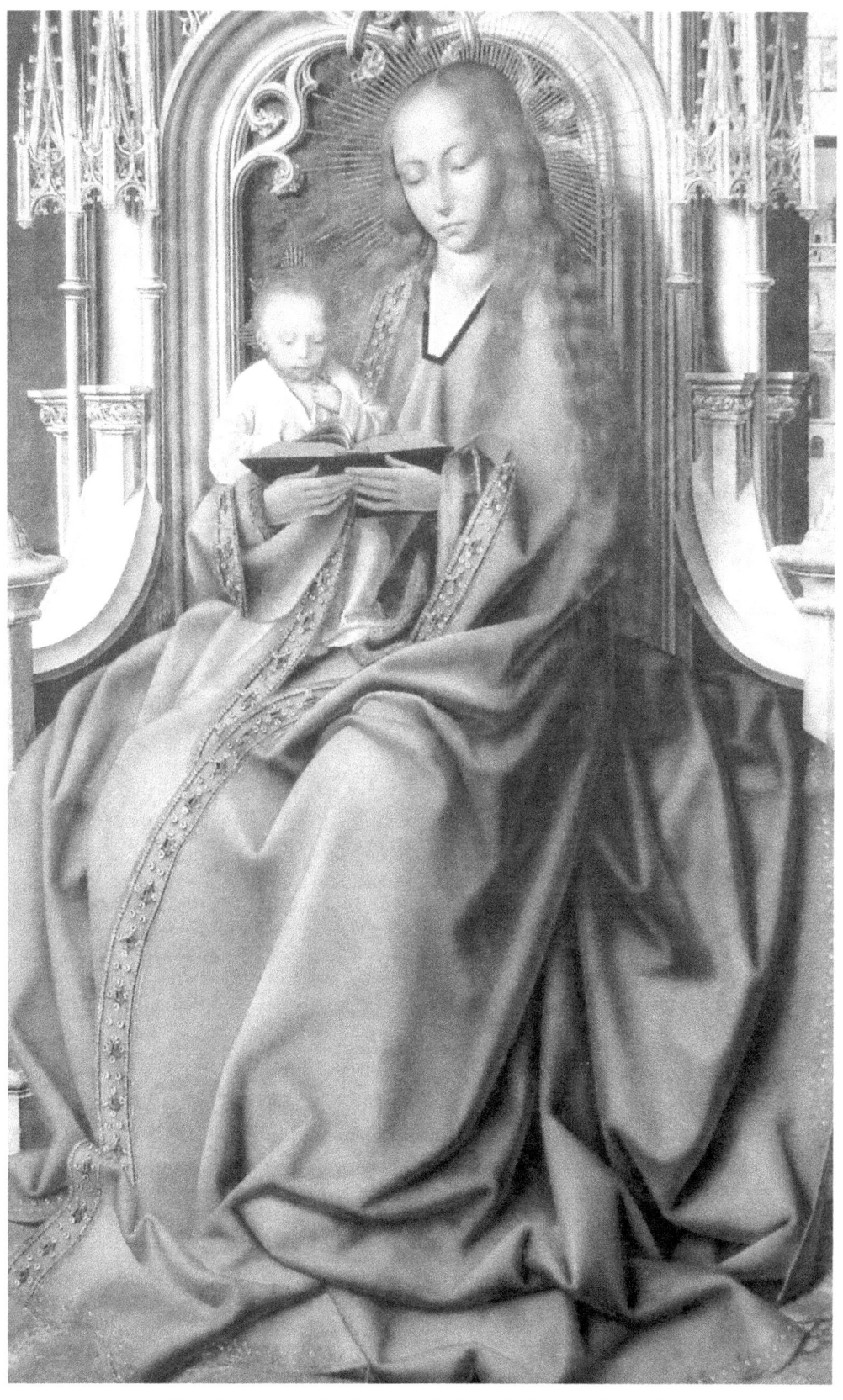

Quentin Massys, Madonna and Child Enthroned, Brussels

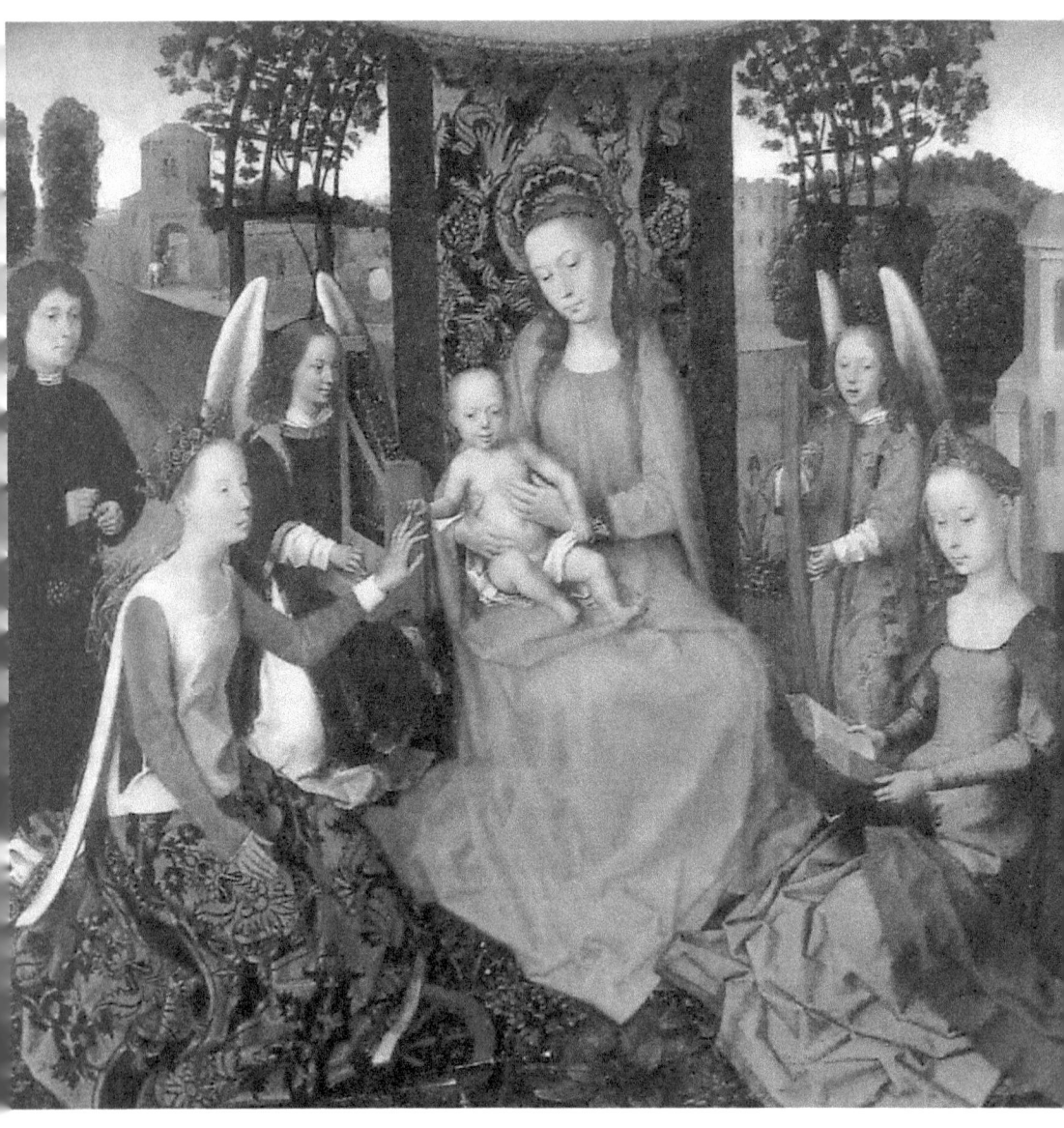

Hans Memling, The Mystic Marriage of St Catherine, Metropolitan
Museum, New York City

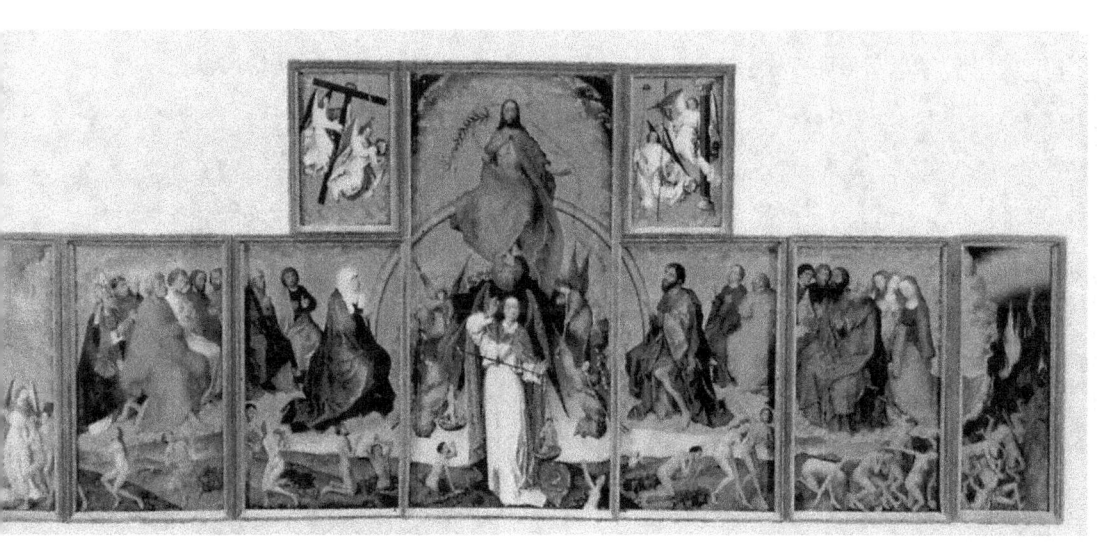

Rogier van der Weyden, The Last Judgement, 1445-49, Beaune

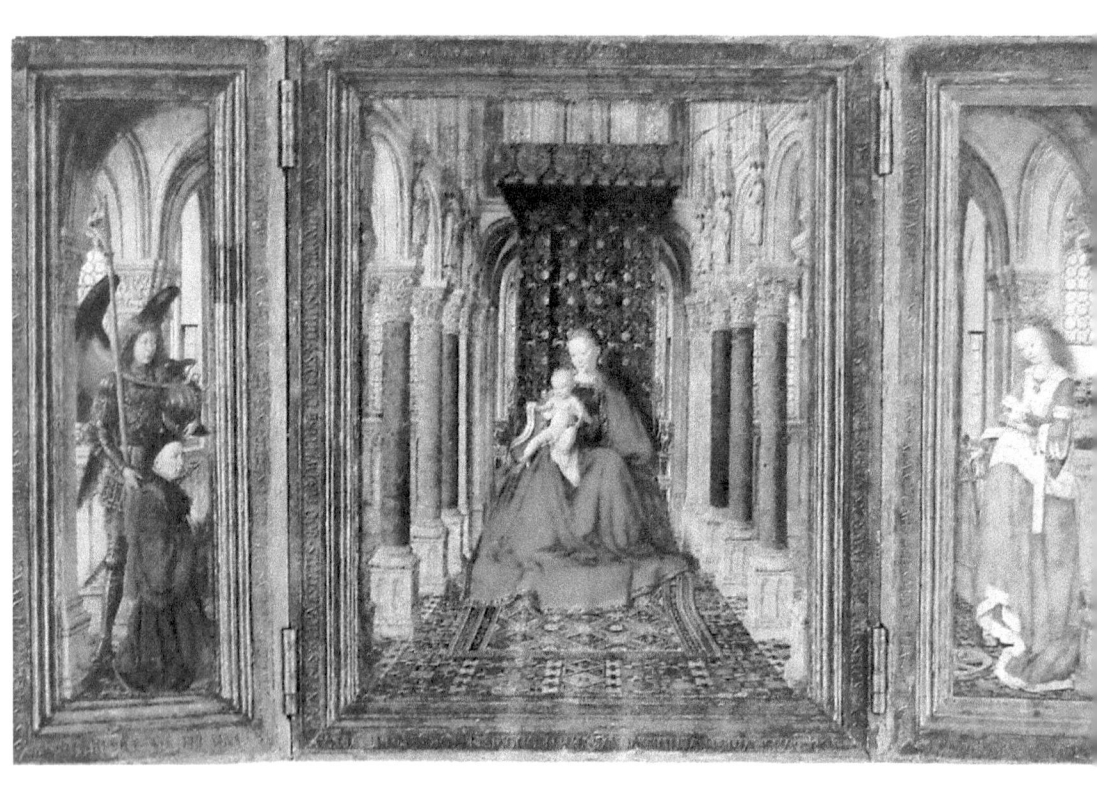

Jan van Eyck, The Dresden Triptych, 1437, Dresden

NOTES ON WORKS

VIRGIN AND CHILD WITH ADORING ANGELS
(In the National Gallery, London)

This is the centre panel from the great altar-piece
commissioned by Duke Lodovico of Milan, from Perugino, for the
Certosa of Pavia, and completed in 1499.

The three lower panels are replaced in the church by copies,
the originals having been purchased from the Certosa by the
Melzi family in 1786, and sold by Duke Melzi to the National
Gallery in 1856. A masterpiece of Pietro's religious art, painted in
his best method and best period.

ST. SEBASTIAN
(In the Musée du Louvre, Paris)

Perugino painted this Saint many times, there being more
than six different renderings still existing. The picture reproduced
here is one of the best, both in the modelling of the nude and the
sentiment of the figure and the lovely Umbrian landscape. It
came (in 1896) from the Sciarra Colonna Gallery. Underneath the
figure will be seen the words, Sagitt? tu? infix? sunt michi.

THE DEPOSITION FROM THE CROSS
(In the Pitti Palace, Florence)

This is the famous painting of the dead Christ for the nuns of S. Chiara, of which Vasari speaks with such enthusiasm, and tells us the nuns were offered (and refused) three times the contract price for the picture.

It certainly is a masterpiece of Italian devotional art. It is fully signed and dated – Petrus Perusinus Pinxit A. D. MCCCCLXXXXV. – and there are studies for it in the Uffizi collection of drawings and at Christ Church, Oxford.

ST. MARY MAGDALEN
(In the Pitti Palace, Florence)

A very lovely figure idealised in type, and recalling, though younger, the Virgin of the great Crucifixion in S. Maria Maddalena dei Pazzi at Florence. Across the bosom, embroidered, runs the legend "S. Maria Maddalena."

VIRGIN WITH LITTLE ST. JOHN ADORING THE INFANT CHRIST
(In the Pitti Palace, Florence)

The centre of the painting is filled by the figure of the Virgin, who, on her knees with hands clasped, adores the little Jesus, seen seated upon a sack, supported by an angel. He is balanced on the other side by the kneeling baby St. John. The Umbrian landscape is of great beauty.

FRANCESCO DELLE OPERE
(In the Uffizi Gallery, Florence)

An interesting portrait, once thought a self-portrait of the master, but now considered to be of Francesco delle Opere. A powerful face, small dark eyes, a well-cut nose, and thick bull-neck. We see that Perugino was a fine portraitist of men, both in this and his genuine self-portrait (in the Sala del Cambio) and the two Vallombrosan monks in the Florence Academy. On the back of this picture is inscribed: 1494 D'Luglio Pietro Perugino Pinse Franco del Ope (i.e. delle Opere).

THE DEAD CHRIST
(In the Academy of Fine Arts, Florence)

Vasari mentions at some length Pietro's work for the Convent of the Gesuati, and in doing so describes this picture: "A Pietà – that is to say, Christ in the lap of Our Lady with four figures around – as good as any painted in his manner." The convent seems to have suffered much from its position without the Porta a Pinti in the siege of Florence, and both this painting and the "Christ in the Garden" eventually found their way to the Academy. Pietro was a good friend of the Gesuati monks, and was a good deal at one time at the convent. Date of this work, about 1493.

VIRGIN AND CHILD WITH TWO MALE SAINTS
(In the National Gallery, London)

This fine painting, very individual in treatment, was painted by Pietro in 1507 for the executors of Giovanni Schiavone, a master-carpenter of Perugia.

In 1822 Baron delle Penna, by whose family it had been inherited, removed the painting to his palace at Perugia, and thence it passed to the London Gallery in 1879.

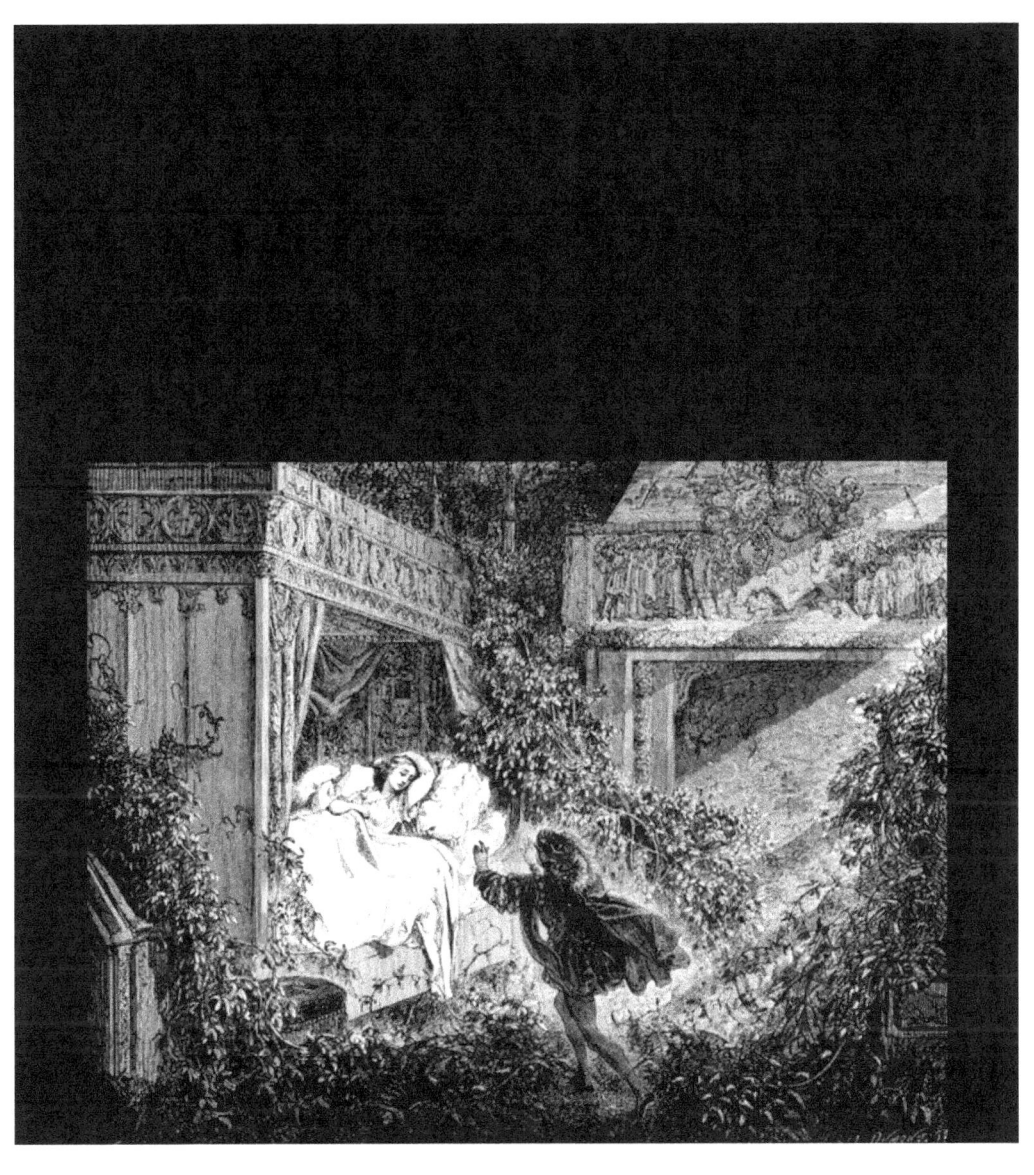

CRESCENT MOON PUBLISHING

web: www.crmoon.com e-mail: cresmopub@yahoo.co.uk

ARTS, PAINTING, SCULPTURE

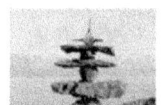
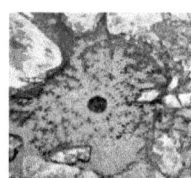
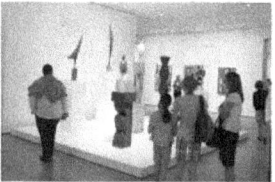
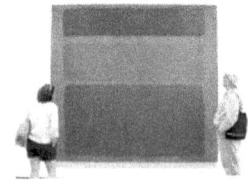

The Art of Andy Goldsworthy
Andy Goldsworthy: Touching Nature
Andy Goldsworthy in Close-Up
Andy Goldsworthy: Pocket Guide
Andy Goldsworthy In America
Land Art: A Complete Guide
The Art of Richard Long
Richard Long: Pocket Guide
Land Art In the UK
Land Art in Close-Up
Land Art In the U.S.A.
Land Art: Pocket Guide
Installation Art in Close-Up
Minimal Art and Artists In the 1960s and After
Colourfield Painting
Land Art DVD, TV documentary
Andy Goldsworthy DVD, TV documentary

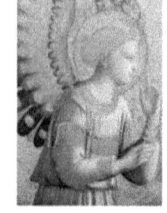

The Erotic Object: Sexuality in Sculpture From Prehistory to the Present Day
Sex in Art: Pornography and Pleasure in Painting and Sculpture
Postwar Art
Sacred Gardens: The Garden in Myth, Religion and Art
Glorification: Religious Abstraction in Renaissance and 20th Century Art
Early Netherlandish Painting
Leonardo da Vinci
Piero della Francesca
Giovanni Bellini

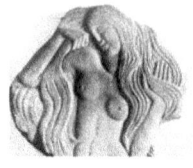
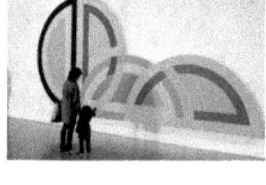

Fra Angelico: Art and Religion in the Renaissance
Mark Rothko: The Art of Transcendence
Frank Stella: American Abstract Artist
Jasper Johns
Brice Marden
Alison Wilding: The Embrace of Sculpture
Vincent van Gogh: Visionary Landscapes
Eric Gill: Nuptials of God

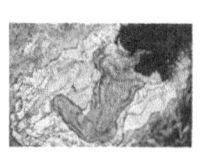
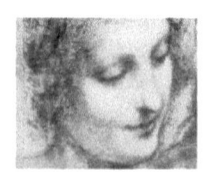

Constantin Brancusi: Sculpting the Essence of Things
Max Beckmann
Caravaggio
Gustave Moreau
Egon Schiele: Sex and Death In Purple Stockings
Delizioso Fotografico Fervore: Works In Process 1
Sacro Cuore: Works In Process 2
The Light Eternal: J.M.W. Turner
The Madonna Glorified: Karen Arthurs

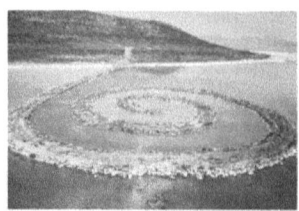

LITERATURE

J.R.R. Tolkien: The Books, The Films, The Whole Cultural Phenomenon
J.R.R. Tolkien: Pocket Guide
Tolkien's Heroic Quest
The *Earthsea* Books of Ursula Le Guin
Beauties, Beasts and Enchantment: Classic French Fairy Tales
German Popular Stories by the Brothers Grimm
Philip Pullman and *His Dark Materials*
Sexing Hardy: Thomas Hardy and Feminism
Thomas Hardy's *Tess of the d'Urbervilles*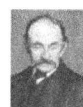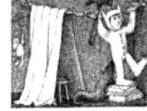
Thomas Hardy's *Jude the Obscure*
Thomas Hardy: The Tragic Novels
Love and Tragedy: Thomas Hardy
The Poetry of Landscape in Hardy
Wessex Revisited: Thomas Hardy and John Cowper Powys
Wolfgang Iser: Essays and Interviews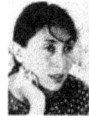
Petrarch, Dante and the Troubadours
Maurice Sendak and the Art of Children's Book Illustration
Andrea Dworkin
Cixous, Irigaray, Kristeva: The *Jouissance* of French Feminism
Julia Kristeva: Art, Love, Melancholy, Philosophy, Semiotics and Psychoanalysis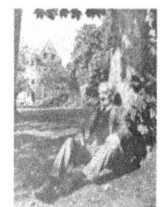
Hélène Cixous I Love You: The *Jouissance* of Writing
Luce Irigaray: Lips, Kissing, and the Politics of Sexual Difference
Peter Redgrove: Here Comes the Flood
Peter Redgrove: Sex-Magic-Poetry-Cornwall
Lawrence Durrell: Between Love and Death, East and West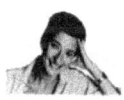
Love, Culture & Poetry: Lawrence Durrell
Cavafy: Anatomy of a Soul
German Romantic Poetry: Goethe, Novalis, Heine, Hölderlin
Feminism and Shakespeare
Shakespeare: Love, Poetry & Magic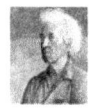
The Passion of D.H. Lawrence
D.H. Lawrence: Symbolic Landscapes
D.H. Lawrence: Infinite Sensual Violence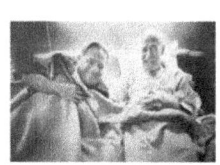
Rimbaud: Arthur Rimbaud and the Magic of Poetry
The Ecstasies of John Cowper Powys
Sensualism and Mythology: The Wessex Novels of John Cowper Powys
Amorous Life: John Cowper Powys and the Manifestation of Affectivity (H.W. Fawkner)
Postmodern Powys: New Essays on John Cowper Powys (Joe Boulter)
Rethinking Powys: Critical Essays on John Cowper Powys
Paul Bowles & Bernardo Bertolucci
Rainer Maria Rilke
Joseph Conrad: *Heart of Darkness*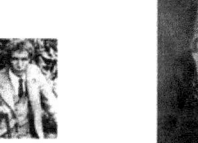
In the Dim Void: Samuel Beckett
Samuel Beckett Goes into the Silence
André Gide: Fiction and Fervour
Jackie Collins and the Blockbuster Novel
Blinded By Her Light: The Love-Poetry of Robert Graves
The Passion of Colours: Travels In Mediterranean Lands
Poetic Forms

POETRY

Ursula Le Guin: Walking In Cornwall
Peter Redgrove: Here Comes The Flood
Peter Redgrove: Sex-Magic-Poetry-Cornwall
Dante: Selections From the Vita Nuova
Petrarch, Dante and the Troubadours
William Shakespeare: Sonnets
William Shakespeare: Complete Poems
Blinded By Her Light: The Love-Poetry of Robert Graves
Emily Dickinson: Selected Poems
Emily Brontë: Poems
Thomas Hardy: Selected Poems
Percy Bysshe Shelley: Poems
John Keats: Selected Poems
Joh n Keats: Poems of 1820
D.H. Lawrence: Selected Poems
Edmund Spenser: Poems
Edmund Spenser: Amoretti
John Donne: Poems
Henry Vaughan: Poems
Sir Thomas Wyatt: Poems
Robert Herrick: Selected Poems
Rilke: Space, Essence and Angels in the Poetry of Rainer Maria Rilke
Rainer Maria Rilke: Selected Poems
Friedrich Hölderlin: Selected Poems
Arseny Tarkovsky: Selected Poems
Arthur Rimbaud: Selected Poems
Arthur Rimbaud: A Season in Hell
Arthur Rimbaud and the Magic of Poetry
Novalis: Hymns To the Night
German Romantic Poetry
Paul Verlaine: Selected Poems
Elizaethan Sonnet Cycles
D.J. Enright: By-Blows
Jeremy Reed: Brigitte's Blue Heart
Jeremy Reed: Claudia Schiffer's Red Shoes
Gorgeous Little Orpheus
Radiance: New Poems
Crescent Moon Book of Nature Poetry
Crescent Moon Book of Love Poetry
Crescent Moon Book of Mystical Poetry
Crescent Moon Book of Elizabethan Love Poetry
Crescent Moon Book of Metaphysical Poetry
Crescent Moon Book of Romantic Poetry
Pagan America: New American Poetry

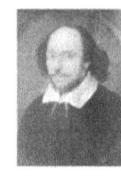
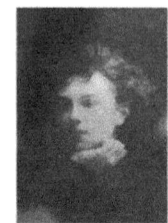
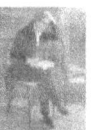
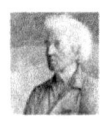
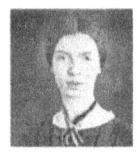
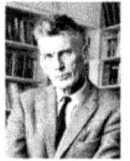
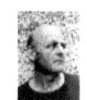
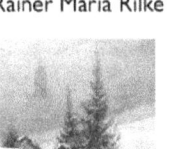
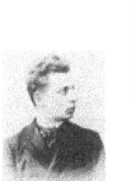
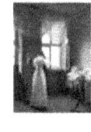
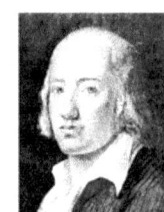
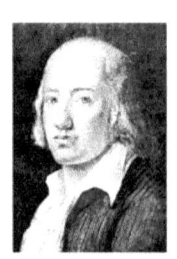

MEDIA, CINEMA, FEMINISM and CULTURAL STUDIES

J.R.R. Tolkien: The Books, The Films, The Whole Cultural Phenomenon
J.R.R. Tolkien: Pocket Guide
The *Lord of the Rings* Movies: Pocket Guide
The Cinema of Hayao Miyazaki
Hayao Miyazaki: *Princess Mononoke*: Pocket Movie Guide
Hayao Miyazaki: *Spirited Away*: Pocket Movie Guide
Tim Burton : Hallowe'en For Hollywood
Ken Russell
Ken Russell: *Tommy*: Pocket Movie Guide

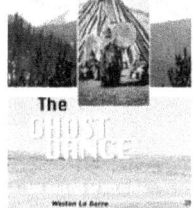

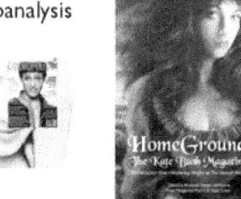

The Ghost Dance: The Origins of Religion
The Peyote Cult
Cixous, Irigaray, Kristeva: The *Jouissance* of French Feminism
Julia Kristeva: Art, Love, Melancholy, Philosophy, Semiotics and Psychoanalysis
Luce Irigaray: Lips, Kissing, and the Politics of Sexual Difference
Hélène Cixous I Love You: The *Jouissance* of Writing
Andrea Dworkin
'Cosmo Woman': The World of Women's Magazines
Women in Pop Music
HomeGround: The Kate Bush Anthology
Discovering the Goddess (Geoffrey Ashe)
The Poetry of Cinema
The Sacred Cinema of Andrei Tarkovsky

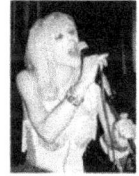

Andrei Tarkovsky: Pocket Guide
Andrei Tarkovsky: *Mirror*: Pocket Movie Guide
Andrei Tarkovsky: *The Sacrifice*: Pocket Movie Guide

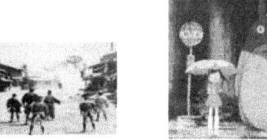

Walerian Borowczyk: Cinema of Erotic Dreams
Jean-Luc Godard: The Passion of Cinema
Jean-Luc Godard: *Hail Mary*: Pocket Movie Guide
Jean-Luc Godard: *Contempt*: Pocket Movie Guide
Jean-Luc Godard: *Pierrot le Fou*: Pocket Movie Guide
John Hughes and Eighties Cinema
Ferris Bueller's Day Off: Pocket Movie Guide

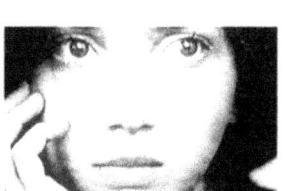

Jean-Luc Godard: Pocket Guide
The Cinema of Richard Linklater
Liv Tyler: Star In Ascendance
Blade Runner and the Films of Philip K. Dick
Paul Bowles and Bernardo Bertolucci
Media Hell: Radio, TV and the Press
An Open Letter to the BBC
Detonation Britain: Nuclear War in the UK
Feminism and Shakespeare
Wild Zones: Pornography, Art and Feminism
Sex in Art: Pornography and Pleasure in Painting and Sculpture
Sexing Hardy: Thomas Hardy and Feminism

The Light Eternal is a model monograph, an exemplary job. The subject matter of the book is beautifully
organised and dead on beam. (Lawrence Durrell)
It is amazing for me to see my work treated with such passion and respect. (Andrea Dworkin)

CRESCENT MOON PUBLISHING
P.O. Box 1312, Maidstone, Kent, ME14 5XU, Great Britain. www.crmoon.com

cresmopub@yahoo.co.uk   www.crescentmoon.org.uk

www.ingramcontent.com/pod-product-compliance
Lightning Source LLC
Chambersburg PA
CBHW051324220526
45468CB00004B/1483